Systematic development of handball offense concepts
Game opening with variants and continuous playing options

Introduction

Dear reader

This is the second time Felix Linden (A-License and certified DHB young talents' coach for competitive areas) gives insights into his understanding of diverse and focused handball training in the book series of handball-uebungen.de. Based on crossing of the center back and the pivot (circle) – which is part of almost every team's repertoire in various forms – Felix Linden explains how you can create different game situations by using simple extensions and hence overcome defense systems with many variants. The individual training units deal with essential elements such as pulling apart a 6-0 defense system, authentic piston movements, pulling out a defense player, different shooting options, and decision-making. All training units focus on decision-making processes in particular. The training units comprise the standard playing structures with continuous playing options on both sides, variants with a second pivot and position switching as well as a variant for outnumbered game situations.

Within the last few years, several counteractive defense measures have been developed in order to interrupt the back position/pivot circle. Consequently, it is important to practice different situations with regard to the back position/pivot circle. The last chapter shows various defense measures and provides an idea of which variants should be played in each situation.

This book contains the following training units:
- Game concept – Crossing of the center back and the pivot – Part 1
- Game concept – Crossing of the center back and the pivot – Part 2
- Game concept – Crossing of the center back and the pivot plus second pivot from the wing position
- Game concept – Crossing of the center back and the pivot plus second pivot from the back position
- Crossing of the center back and the pivot in outnumbered situations

Difficulty levels of the training units:
- ★ Simple requirement (all youth and adult teams)
- ★★ Intermediate requirement (youth teams under 15 years of age and adult teams)
- ★★★ Higher requirement (youth teams under 17 years of age and adult teams)
- ★★★★ Highest requirement (competitive area)

Table of contents:

Introduction

1. Training units
   - No. 1: Game concept – Crossing of the center back and the pivot – Part 1
   - No. 2: Game concept – Crossing of the center back and the pivot – Part 2
   - No. 3: Game concept – Crossing of the center back and the pivot plus second pivot from the wing position
   - No. 4: Game concept – Crossing of the center back and the pivot second pivot from the back position
   - No. 5: Crossing of the center back and the pivot in outnumbered situations

2. Counteractive measures to be expected and appropriate reactions

3. About the editors

4. Further books published by DV Concept

Thanks go to the first ladies' handball team and the male under-19 handball team of ATV Biesel for their active support during the training units.

Felix Linden will donate parts of the revenue to the charity "United Smile e.V.". With his charity, Jens Dauben, a dentist and one of Felix Linden's players, supports children and adults in remote regions of the world who do not have access to dental and medical standard care.

Publishing information
1st English edition released on 28 Aug 2018
German original edition released on 07 Jun 2018

Published by DV Concept
Editors: Felix Linden, Jörg Madinger
Design and layout: Jörg Madinger, Elke Lackner
Pictures: Gisbert Schlemmer
Proofreading and English translation: Nina-Maria Nahlenz

ISBN: 978-3-95641-217-2

This publication is listed in the catalogue of the **German National Library**. Please refer to http://dnb.de for bibliographic data.

The work and its components are protected by copyright. No reprinting, photomechanical reproduction, storing or processing in electronic systems without the publisher's written permission.

Systematic development of handball offense concepts
Game opening with variants and continuous playing options

1. Training units

No. 1	Game concept – Crossing of the center back and the pivot – Part 1			★★★	90
Opening part		**Main part**			
X	Warm-up/Stretching		Offense/Individual	Jumping power	
	Running exercise	X	Offense/Small groups	Sprint contest	
	Short game	X	Offense/Team	Goalkeeper	
	Coordination	X	Offense/Series of shots		
	Coordination run		Defense/Individual	**Final part**	
	Strengthening		Defense/Small groups	Closing game	
X	Ball familiarization		Defense/Team	Final sprint	
X	Goalkeeper warm-up shooting		Athletics		
			Endurance		

Key:

✗   Cone

△1   Attacking player

●1   Defense player

▣   Ball box

▬   Foam noodles (foam beams)

▢   Upper part of a large vaulting box

Equipment required:
→ 2 foam noodles (foam beams) 1 upper part of a large vaulting box, 2 cones, 2 ball boxes with sufficient number of handballs

Description:
Following warm-up with two ball familiarization exercises, this training unit introduces crossing of the center back and the pivot as the basic action already during the goalkeeper warm-up shooting and a subsequent series of shots. Afterwards, the players practice how to make decisions when the ball is passed to the back position players. This is followed by a further small group exercise and eventually the final team exercise during which the players should directly implement a first variant when playing the initial pass.

The training unit consists of the following key exercises:
- Warm-up/Stretching (individual exercise: 10 minutes/total time: 10 minutes)
- Ball familiarization (10/20)
- Ball familiarization (10/30)
- Goalkeeper warm-up shooting (10/40)
- Offense/Series of shots (15/55)
- Offense/Small groups (10/65)
- Offense/Small groups (15/80)
- Offense/Team (10/90)

Training unit total time: 90 Min.

Systematic development of handball offense concepts
Game opening with variants and continuous playing options

No.: 1-1	Warm-up/Stretching	10	10

Course:

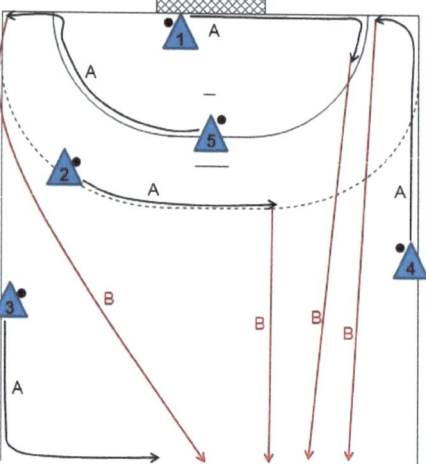

- The players each have a ball and run along the lines on the court floor (A).
- While doing this, they perform different running moves as instructed by the coach:
    - Dribbling the ball with the right/left hand.
    - Dribbling the ball with the right/left hand alternately.
    - Sidestepping while dribbling the ball.
    - Hopping and handing over the ball from the right to the left hand (and back) above the head.

(Figure 1)

- Running backward and moving the ball around the hips in circles (see figure).
- The coach whistles after a while and defines a target which the players must touch (e.g. goal post, center line (B), a corner of the playing field, a green line, something red (not worn by the player himself) etc.).

(Figure 2)

- The players sprint and try to fulfill the task as fast as possible.
- The last player must fulfill an extra task (10 quick jumping jacks, 10 push-ups etc.).
- Afterwards, the players perform stretching/mobilization exercises together.

Systematic development of handball offense concepts
Game opening with variants and continuous playing options

No.: 1-2	Ball familiarization	10	20

Setting:

- The players stand in a circle, (c) has a ball and stands in the center of the circle.

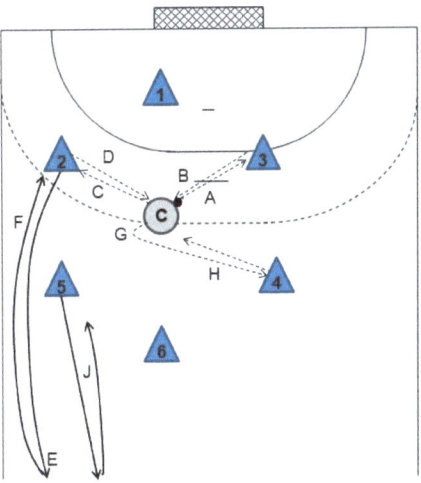

Course:

- (c) plays double passes with the players (A, B, C, and D).
- Before a player may receive a ball (A), he must clap his hands one time, then catch the ball, and pass it back again (B).
- If a player misses to clap, or if a player fails to catch the ball, he must sprint to the center line (E) and back (F).
- (c) may also feint a pass (G) and pass to another player instead (H).
- If a player claps even though he does not get the ball, he must also sprint to the center line (J).

Variant:

- Instead of (c), one of the players undertakes the task in the center.
- For large groups, divide the players into two smaller groups.

⚠ (c) (or the player in the center) should try to fool the players standing in the circle as often as possible.

No.: 1-3	Ball familiarization	10	30

Setting:
- Define the running path with cones.

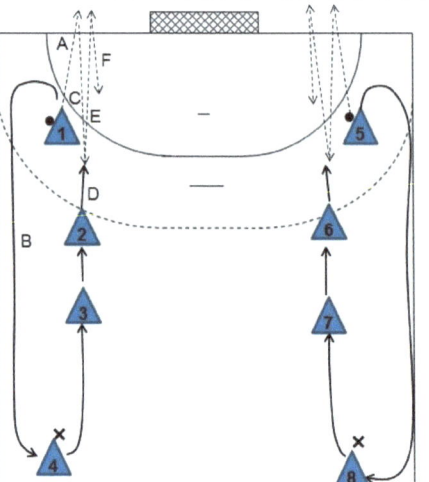

Course:
- 1 bounces the ball against the gym wall (A) and afterwards runs around the remote cone (B).
- 2 catches (D) the ball bouncing back from the wall (C), immediately throws it against the wall as well (E), and also runs around the cone.
- 3 catches the ball bouncing back from the wall (F), and so on.

⚠ Position the cone in such a way that the players can start the next round shortly after they ran around the cone and do not have to wait before catching the ball. For larger groups, divide the players into several groups.

⚠ The players should bounce the ball against the wall in different variants:
- Bounce it against the wall directly and catch it directly.
- Bounce it against the wall indirectly (bounce pass) and catch it indirectly (after it bounced on the floor one time).
- Bounce it against the wall indirectly and catch it directly.

Systematic development of handball offense concepts
Game opening with variants and continuous playing options

| No.: 1-4 | Goalkeeper warm-up shooting | 10 | 40 |

Setting:
- Define the starting position of the pivot as well as the shooting corridor with two foam noodles (foam beams).

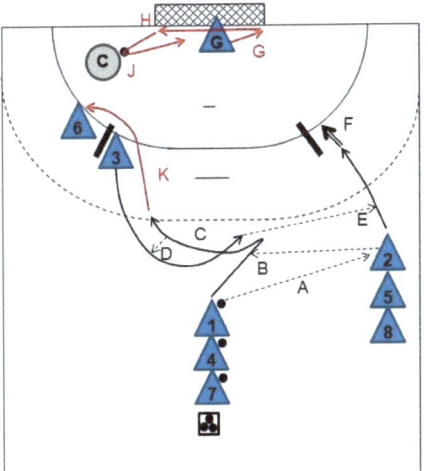

Course:
- ▲1 plays the initial pass to ▲2 (A), makes a slight piston movement to the right, and receives a return pass (B).
- ▲1 clearly moves to the left (C) (he may bounce the ball one time with the hand that is not in direction of the defense).
- ▲3 starts from the pivot position, crosses behind ▲1 (D), and receives a pass.
- ▲3 moves far to the right and passes the ball into the parallel running path of ▲2 (E), who runs along the beam on the right side and eventually shoots at the right side of the goal as instructed (hands, top, bottom) (F).
- The goalkeeper starts from the center of the goal and tries to save the shot (G).
- ▲4 starts the next course with ▲6 as the pivot and ▲5 as the shooting player.
- After the shot, G turns around and alternately touches the goalposts and the cross bar three times with the right hand with his back turned to the goal. Afterwards, he runs to the left side, touches the left goalpost (H), turns around, immediately sprints to C, and touches the ball presented (J). Subsequently, G moves back to the center of the goal in order to save the next shot.
- ▲1 lines up for the pivot position after the crossing (K), ▲3 moves to the right back position, and the shooting players line up for the center back position, each holding a ball.

⚠ The intermediate task for G should be fulfilled in such a way that there is no waiting time between the shots, neither for the goalkeeper nor for the shooting players.

⚠ The players should repeat the course on the other side as well and shoot from the left back position.

Systematic development of handball offense concepts
Game opening with variants and continuous playing options

No.: 1-5	Offense/Series of shots	15	55

Setting:

- Define the starting position of the pivot as well as the shooting corridor for the pivot with two foam noodles (foam beams).
- Position the upper part of a large vaulting box as shown in the figure for the shot from the right back position.

Course:

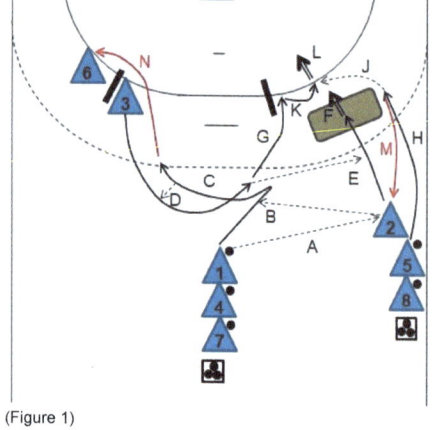

(Figure 1)

- ▲1 plays the initial pass to ▲2 (A), makes a slight piston movement to the right, and receives a return pass (B).
- ▲1 clearly moves to the left (C) (he may bounce the ball one time with the hand that is not in direction of the defense).
- ▲3 starts as the pivot, crosses behind ▲1 (D), and receives a pass.
- ▲3 moves far to the right and passes the ball into the parallel running path of ▲2 (E), who steps onto the upper part of the vaulting box and makes a jump shot at the goal (see figure 2) (F).

(Figure 2)

- After the pass, ▲3 immediately moves to the pivot position (G) and places a screen next to the foam beam.
- ▲5 makes a piston movement towards the goal immediately after the shot of ▲2 (H), and plays a pass around the upper part of the vaulting box into the space at the 6-meter zone (J).
- ▲3 catches the ball (K) and shoots from the pivot position (L).
- ▲4 immediately starts the subsequent course with ▲6 as the pivot and ▲5 as the shooting player, who moves backward immediately after he played the pass (M).
- ▲1 lines up for the pivot position (N), ▲3 moves to the right back position, and the shooting players on the right back position line up for the center back position, each holding a ball.

Systematic development of handball offense concepts
Game opening with variants and continuous playing options

⚠ The shooting back position players must time their running movement in such a way that they make their last step allowed onto the upper part of the vaulting box and do a jump shot without reducing their speed.

⚠ The players should repeat the course on the other side as well and shoot from the left back position.

No.: 1-6	Offense/Small groups	10	65

Setting:
- Define the playing field for the 3-on-2 game with foam beams.

Course:
- ① plays the initial pass to ② (A), makes a slight piston movement to the right, and receives a return pass (B).
- ① clearly moves to the left (C) (he may bounce the ball one time with the hand that is not in direction of the defense).
- ③ starts as the pivot, crosses behind ① (D), and receives a pass.
- If there is a large gap next to ①, ③ may approach the goal directly (E).
- Usually, ③ passes the ball into the parallel piston move of ② (F).
- ② approaches the defense at full speed and initially tries to break through (G).
- If ② closes the gap (H), ② passes the ball to the wing player ④ (J), and ④ shoots at the goal (K). Alternatively, ② may pass the ball back to the pivot ③ (not shown in the figure), if ① closes the gap.
- ① lines up for the pivot position, ③ moves to the right back position, ② lines up for the center back position with a ball, ④ keeps his position or takes turns with a second defense player.

⚠ ② should approach the goal during the 3-on-2 play and try to break through before passing the ball to the pivot or to the wing position player.

⚠ The players should repeat the course on the other side as well and play 3-on-2 on the left side.

⚠ Switch the defense players at regular intervals.

No.: 1-7 — Offense/Small groups — 15 — 80

Setting:
- Define the playing fields with two foam beams.

Course:
- 3 plays the initial pass to 4 (A), makes a slight piston movement to the right, and receives a return pass (B).
- 3 clearly moves to the left (C) (he may bounce the ball one time with the hand that is not in direction of the defense).
- 6 starts as the pivot, crosses behind 3 (D), and receives a pass (variant 1; figure 1).

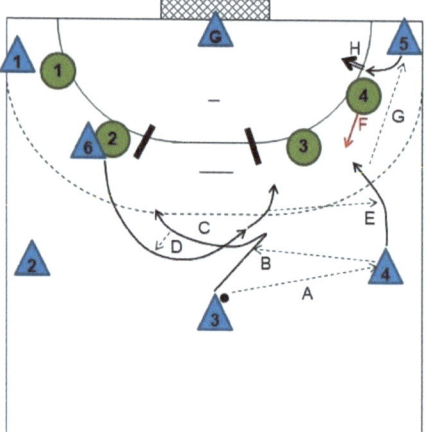

Figure 1

- 6 passes the ball into the parallel piston move of 4 (E). Subsequently, the players keep on playing 3-on-2 in the right playing corridor until they have shot at the goal (F, G, and H).
- After the crossing, 3 may – instead of passing the ball into the crossing movement of 6 – also pass the ball into the parallel piston move of 2 (J) on the left side (variant 2; figure 2).

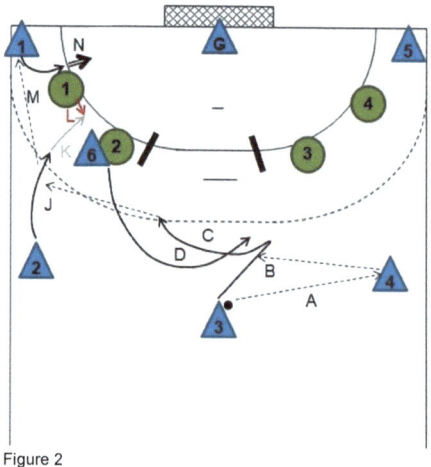

Figure 2

- 2 approaches the goal and tries to break through (K).
- If 1 closes the gap (L), 2 passes the ball to the wing player 1 (M), who then shoots at the goal (N).

⚠ 3 must decide which variant will be played, depending on the position of 2.

⚠ 2 must anticipate the parallel pass at any time and start to run accordingly.

⚠ The back position players should approach the goal and try to break through before passing the ball.

⚠ Switch the defense players at regular intervals.

Systematic development of handball offense concepts
Game opening with variants and continuous playing options

No.: 1-8	Offense/Team	10	90

Setting:
- Divide the field longitudinally into a right and left half.

Course:
- The players play 6-on-6. They should always open the game with the course practiced before.
- 3 plays the initial pass to 4 (A), makes a slight piston movement to the right, and receives a return pass (B).
- 3 clearly moves to the left (C) (he may bounce the ball one time with the hand that is not in direction of the defense).
- 6 starts from the pivot position and crosses behind 3.
- 3 now decides on which half will be played:
    - If 3 passes into the crossing movement of 6 (D), 6 passes to 4 (E), and 4, 5, and 6 play freely on the right side until one of the players has shot at the goal (F, G, and H).
    - If 3 passes into the piston movement path of 2 (J), 2, 1, and 3 play on the left side until one of the players has shot at the goal (K and L). 6 runs to the other side but does not take action.
- Each team plays 10 attacks, with five initial passes each to the left and to the right side and continuous playing depending on the decision of 3.
- Switch tasks afterwards. Which team has shot the most goals?

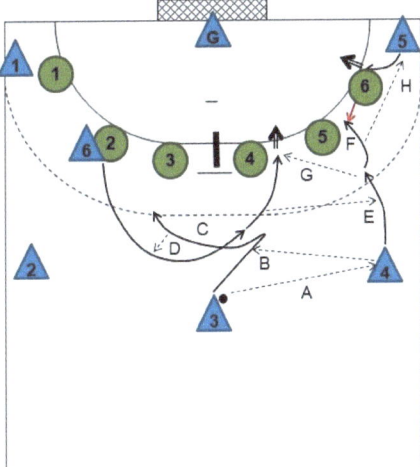

Figure 1

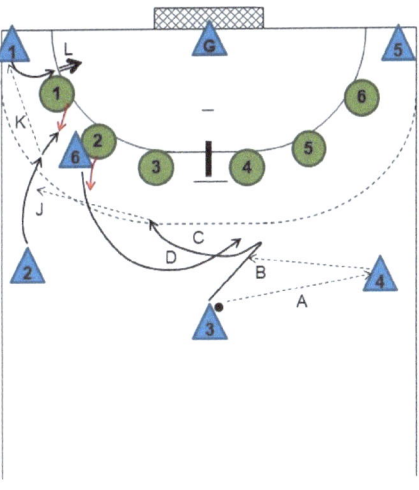

Figure 2

No. 2	Game concept – Crossing of the center back and the pivot – Part 2			★★★	90
	Opening part		**Main part**		
X	Warm-up/Stretching		Offense/Individual		Jumping power
	Running exercise	X	Offense/Small groups		Sprint contest
	Short game	X	Offense/Team		Goalkeeper
	Coordination	X	Offense/Series of shots		
	Coordination run		Defense/Individual		**Final part**
X	Strengthening		Defense/Small groups		Closing game
	Ball familiarization		Defense/Team		Final sprint
X	Goalkeeper warm-up shooting		Athletics		
			Endurance		

Key:

✗ Cone

△ Attacking player

● Defense player

⬛ Ball box

▬ Foam noodles (foam beams)

▭ Small vaulting box

Equipment required:
➔ 4 cones,
4 small vaulting boxes,
2 foam beams (foam noodles), ball box with sufficient number of handballs, poster with exercises

Description:
Following warm-up and course strength trainings, this training unit again focuses on the standard crossing variant of the center back and the pivot during the goalkeeper warm-up shooting. After a series of shots from the wing and pivot positions, this will be extended by a long pass on the back positions. Subsequently, the decision-making process of the back position player after receiving the long pass is paramount; at the same time, the players develop two playing variants.

The training unit consists of the following key exercises:
- Warm-up/Stretching (individual exercise: 10 minutes/total time: 10 minutes)
- Strengthening (10/20)
- Goalkeeper warm-up shooting (15/35)
- Offense/Series of shots (10/45)
- Offense/Small groups (10/55)
- Offense/Small groups (10/65)
- Offense/Small groups (15/80)
- Offense/Team (10/90)

Training unit total time: 90 min.

Systematic development of handball offense concepts
Game opening with variants and continuous playing options

No.: 2-1	Warm-up/Stretching	10	10

Setting:
- Define a rectangle or a square with cones.

Course 1:
- The teams initially make groups of 2.
- The coach gives the following instructions for each round:
    - Running forward, arm rotation in opposite directions (forward/backward)
    - Running backward, forward/backward arm rotation etc.

  as well as a topic of conversation:
    - Was there anything special today regarding everyday life?
    - How did you start the day?
    - What did you do right before the training?
- The groups of 2 run around the cones next to each other (A and B) and talk about the topic specified.
- After one round, the coach gives the next instruction and topic of conversation.
- The players make new groups of 2 and run another round.
- Afterwards, the players perform stretching/mobilization exercises together.

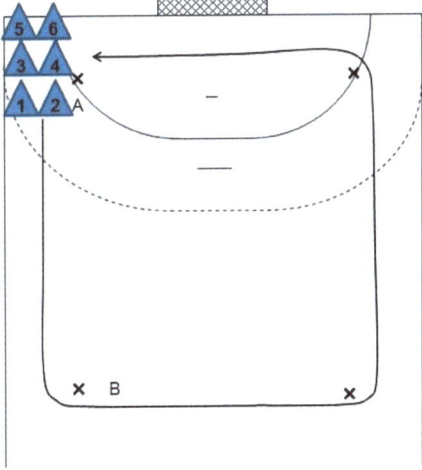

(Figure 1)

(Figure 2)

| No.: 2-2 | Strengthening | 10 | 20 |

Setting:
- Position cones and small vaulting boxes as shown in the figure. (Position small gym mats for the strengthening exercises, if applicable.)
- Write down exercises on a poster (A).
- Divide the players into three groups and allocate a starting point to each group.

Course:
- The players do the exercises on the poster one after the other (A). Each group starts at their respective starting point.
- The players must sign off each exercise performed until each player has fulfilled each task.

Tasks:
- Sprinting 3 times around the rectangle defined with cones (B).
- Running around the rectangle defined with cones (B).
- Stepping on a vaulting box 10 times with one leg and moving up the other leg towards the elbow (C) (see figure 2).
- Stepping on the vaulting box 6 times and jumping off the box with straight legs (toes facing upwards) (D) (see figure 3).
- Six burpees (E)
- 10 crunches (F)

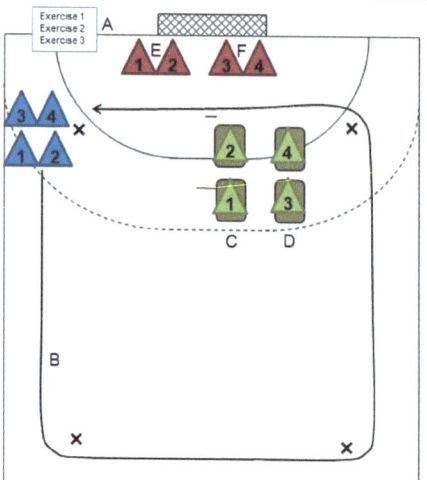
(Figure 1)

(Figure 2)   (Figure 3)

Systematic development of handball offense concepts
Game opening with variants and continuous playing options

| No.: 2-3 | Goalkeeper warm-up shooting | 15 | 35 |

Course 1 (figure 1):

- **1** passes the ball to **2** (A), makes a slight piston movement to the right, and receives a return pass (B).

- **1** clearly moves to the left (C) (he may bounce the ball one time with the hand that is not in direction of the defense).

- **3** starts as the pivot, crosses behind **1**, and receives a pass (D).

- **3** passes to **2** into his running move (E) and **2** shoots at the left side of the goal as instructed (top, middle, bottom) (F).

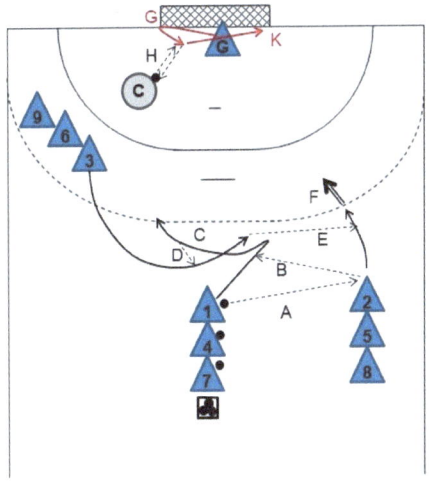

(Figure 1)

- During the crossing, **G** touches the left goalpost (G), plays a double pass with **c** (H), and then saves the shot to the right (K).

- Afterwards, the next three players start the course (**1** lines up for the pivot position, **2** lines up for the center back position, and **3** lines up for the right back position).

Course 2 (figures 2 and 3):

- The initial action (A to D) remains the same as in course 1.

- **3** passes the ball to **2** into his running movement (E).

- **1** moves to the 6-meter line after the crossing and becomes a defense player of the defensive block (F).

- During the crossing, **G** touches the right goalpost (G), plays a double pass with **c** (H), and moves back to the center of the goal (J).

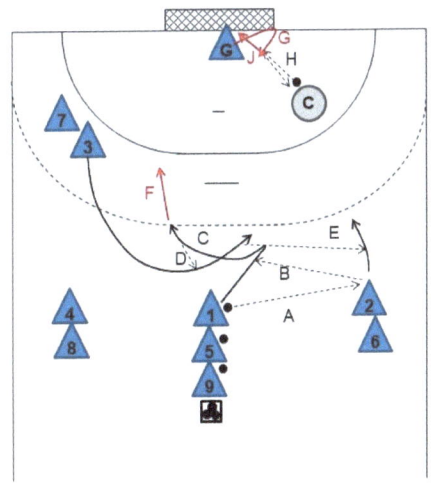

(Figure 2)

Systematic development of handball offense concepts
Game opening with variants and continuous playing options

- ▲2 passes the ball (K) to the left back position player into the running path of ▲4 (L).
- ▲4 shoots over the block of ▲1 (M); ▲G works together with the defense block player and tries to save the shot (N).

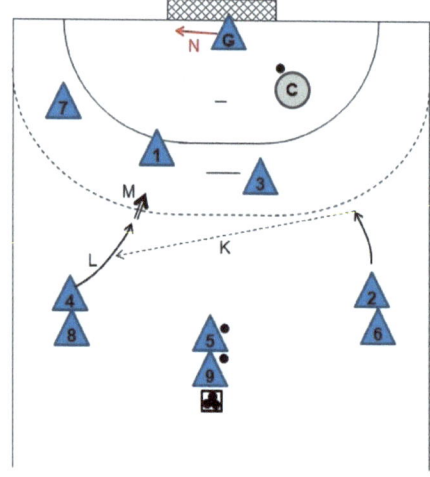

(Figure 3)

Systematic development of handball offense concepts
Game opening with variants and continuous playing options

| No.: 2-4 | Offense/Series of shots | 10 | 45 |

Course:

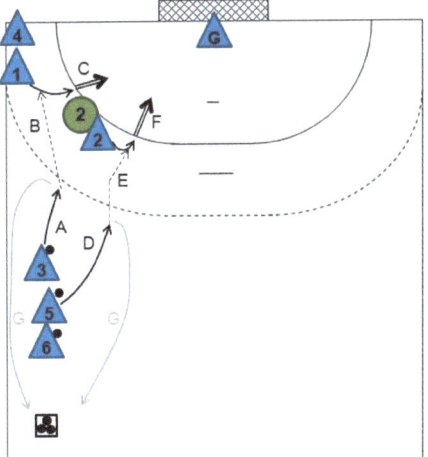

- 3 starts to run with the ball (A) and passes it to the wing player 1 (B) into his running movement.
- 1 shoots at the goal (C).
- Afterwards, 5 starts with the ball, slightly moves towards the center (D), and plays a bounce pass to 2 on the pivot position (E).
- 2 shoots at the goal (F).
- Repeat the course; 6 starts with the ball, passes it to the wing player, and 4 shoots.
- Then the pivot shoots again, and so on.
- Immediately after playing the pass, the back position players move backward (G), pick up another ball from the ball box and line up again for the back position.
- The wing players line up again for the wing position; the pivot shoots several times in a row alternating with the wing player.

Competition:
- One player shoots from the pivot position, several players shoot from the wing position.
- There is always one shot from the wing position and one shot from the pivot position alternately.
- Who has scored more goals – the wing players or the pivot?
- As soon as each wing player has shot one time, repeat the course with a new pivot.

⚠ Also do the series of shots on the right side.

Systematic development of handball offense concepts
Game opening with variants and continuous playing options

No.: 2-5	Offense/Small groups	10	55

Setting:
- Define the playing field of the pivot with a foam beam.

Course:

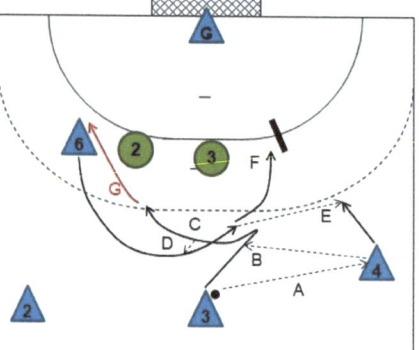
(Figure 1)

- ▲3 plays the initial pass to ▲4 (A), makes a slight piston movement to the right, and receives a return pass (B).

- ▲3 clearly moves to the left (C) (he may bounce the ball one time with the hand that is not in direction of the defense).

- ▲6 starts as the pivot, crosses behind ▲3, and receives a pass (D). ▲3 moves to the 6-meter line (G).

- ▲6 passes the ball to ▲4 into his piston movement (E) and afterwards moves to the 6-meter line (F).

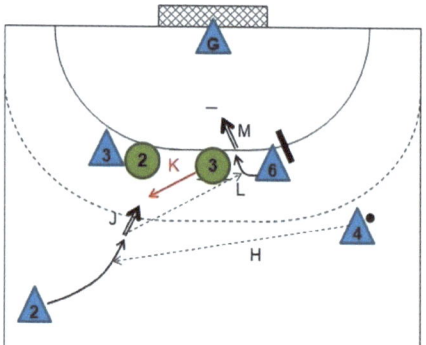
(Figure 2)

- ▲2 runs a slight curve towards the center and receives a pass from ▲4 into his running path (H).

- ▲2 must decide now:
    o If the defense players act defensively, ▲2 shoots from the back position (J).
    o If ●3 makes a step forward towards ▲2 (K), ▲2 passes the ball to the pivot ▲6 (L), and ▲6 eventually shoots at the goal (M).

- Afterwards, the course starts over with new back position players and a new pivot.

⚠ ●3 should vary his defense behavior so that the back position player faces different situations and must adapt his decisions accordingly.

⚠ Switch the defense players at regular intervals.

⚠ The players should repeat the course on the other side with the right back position player as decision-maker.

Systematic development of handball offense concepts
Game opening with variants and continuous playing options

No.: 2-6	Offense/Small groups	10	65

Setting:
- Define the playing field of the pivot with a foam beam.

Course:

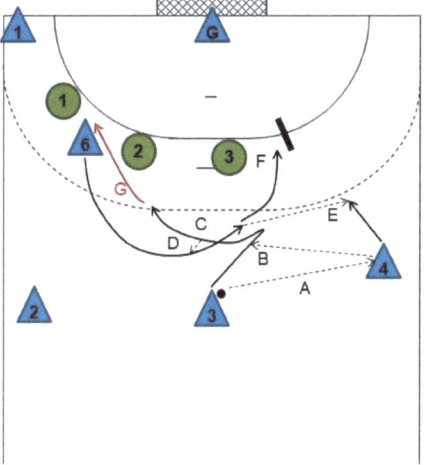

- 3 plays the initial pass to 4 (A), makes a slight piston movement to the right, and receives a return pass (B).
- 3 clearly moves to the left (C) (he may bounce the ball one time with the hand that is not in direction of the defense).
- 6 starts as the pivot, crosses behind 3, and receives a pass (D).

Figure 1

- 6 passes the ball to 4 into his piston movement (E) and afterwards moves to the 6-meter line (F).
- 3 stands on the other side, also at the 6-meter line (G).
- 2 runs a slight curve towards the center and receives a pass from 4 into his running path (H).
- 2 must decide now:

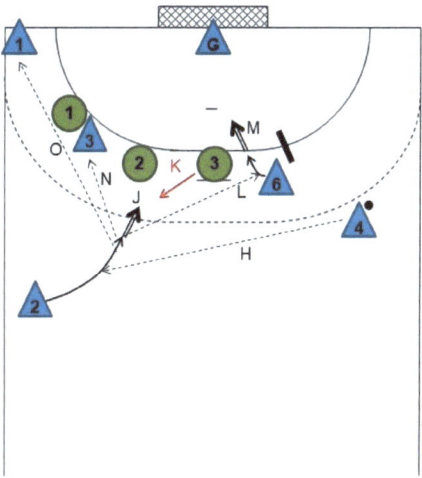

  - If the defense players remain defensive, 2 shoots from the back position (J).

Figure 2

  - If 3 makes a step forward towards 2 (K), 2 passes the ball to the pivot 6 (L), and 6 eventually shoots at the goal (M).
  - If 2 prevents the shot and 3 covers 6, 2 may interact with 3 on the pivot position (N) or with 1 on the wing position (O), depending on the defense behavior of 1.
- Afterwards, the course starts over with five new attacking players.

Systematic development of handball offense concepts
Game opening with variants and continuous playing options

⚠ The defense players should vary their defense behavior so that the back position player faces different situations and must adapt his decisions accordingly.

⚠ Switch the defense players at regular intervals.

⚠ The players should repeat the course on the other side with the right back position player as decision-maker.

No.: 2-7	Offense/Small groups	15	80

Setting:
- Define the playing field with two foam noodles (foam beams).

Course:
- ③ plays the initial pass to ④ (A), makes a slight piston movement to the right, and receives a return pass (B).
- ③ clearly moves to the left (C) (he may bounce the ball one time with the hand that is not in direction of the defense).
- ⑥ starts as the pivot, crosses behind ③ (D), and receives a pass.
- If there is a large gap next to ①, ⑥ may approach the goal directly (not shown in the figure).
- Usually, ⑥ passes the ball into the parallel piston move of ④ (E). If possible, ④ breaks through to the 6-meter line (not shown in the figure).
- After the parallel pass, ⑥ approaches the 6-meter line (F).

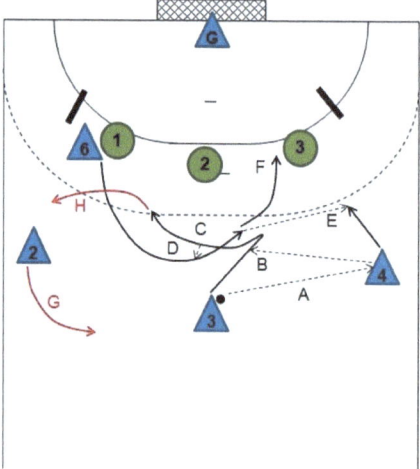

(Figure 1)

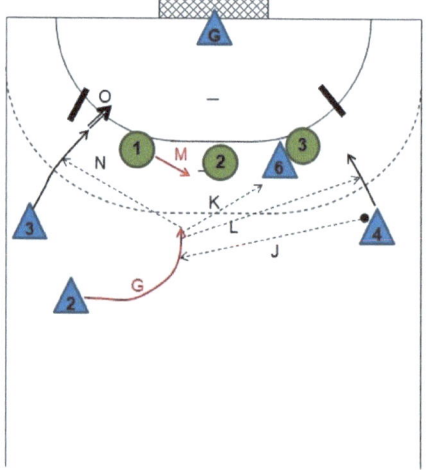

(Figure 2)

- **3** moves back to the right back position after the crossing (H).
- **2** makes up for the center (G).
- **4** passes the ball to **2** into his running path (J) and **2** must make a decision, depending on the behavior of the defense players:
    - If the defense players remain defensive, **2** may shoot from the back position.
    - Depending on the position of **3**, **2** may pass the ball to the pivot (K) or back to **4** (L).
    - If **1** moves along with the attacking player (M), **2** passes the ball to **3** (N), and **3** breaks through and eventually shoots at the goal (O).

Competition:
- Three players start as the defense players, the remaining players make teams of 4 for the attack and compete with each other (if applicable, the pivot may join several or all teams of 4 in the attacks).
- The teams of 4 must always initiate their attack with the course practiced before. After the crossing with the pivot, the players may keep on playing freely.
- Which team of 4 scores highest? The players of the winning team each get a point.
- Afterwards, substitute the defense players and make new teams of 4.
- Who has scored highest in the end?

Systematic development of handball offense concepts
Game opening with variants and continuous playing options

No.: 2-8	Offense/Team		10	90

Course:

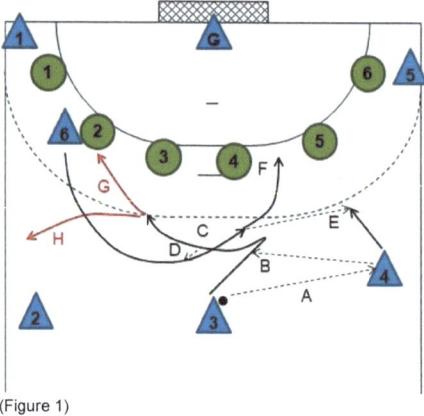

- The players play 6-on-6 and should implement the variants practiced before during the training unit.
- The attacking players and the defense players switch tasks after 10 attacks.
- 3 passes the ball to 4 (A), makes a piston movement to the right, and receives a return pass (B).

(Figure 1)

- 3 clearly moves to the left (C) (he may bounce the ball one time).
- 6 starts as the pivot, crosses behind 3 (D), and receives a pass.
- 6 passes the ball into the parallel piston move of 4 (E). If possible, 4 breaks through to the 6-meter line (not shown in the figure).
- After the parallel pass, 6 approaches the 6-meter line (F).
- Depending on the variant played, 3 acts as a second pivot (G) or moves back to the left back position (H).

Variant 1: Playing with a second pivot (figure 2):

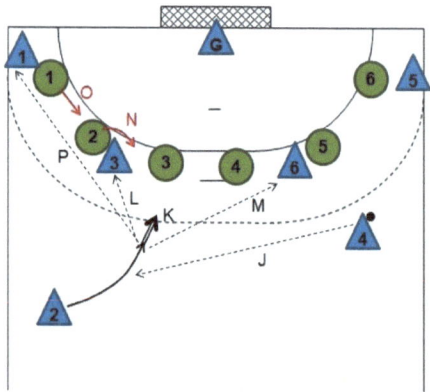

- 2 runs a curve towards the center and receives a pass from 4 (J).
- 2 must decide now:
  - If the defense players remain defensive, 2 shoots from the back position (K).

(Figure 2)

  - If 3 makes a step forward towards 2, 2 passes the ball to the pivot 3 (L).
  - If 4 moves to the inner side, 6 may receive a pass (M).
  - If 2 runs around 3 on the pivot position (N) and 1 moves to the inner side (O), 2 passes the ball to the wing player (P).

Systematic development of handball offense concepts
Game opening with variants and continuous playing options

Variant 2: Continuous playing with a single pivot (figure 3):

- **2** runs a shorter curve towards the center and receives a pass from **4** (J).
- If the defense players remain defensive, **2** shoots (K).
- If the defense players move to the inner side (L), the attacking players may try to achieve numerical superiority on the left wing position (M/N, O/P).
- If the defense players move to the left, **4** receives a return pass (Q), and the attacking players keep on playing freely.

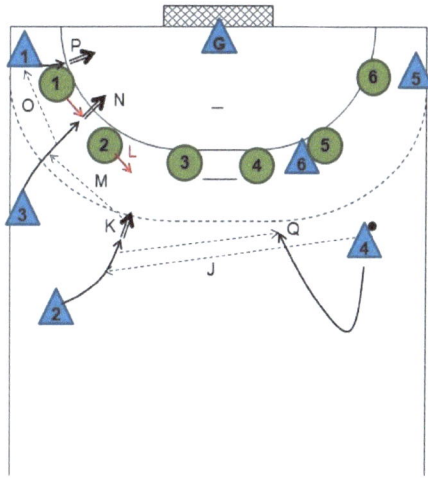

(Figure 3)

Notes:
_____
_____
_____
_____
_____
_____
_____
_____
_____

No. 3	Game concept – Crossing of the center back and the pivot plus second pivot from the wing position		★★★	90
	Opening part		Main part	
X	Warm-up/Stretching		Offense/Individual		Jumping power
	Running exercise	X	Offense/Small groups	X	Sprint contest
X	Short game	X	Offense/Team		Goalkeeper
	Coordination	X	Offense/Series of shots		
	Coordination run		Defense/Individual		**Final part**
	Strengthening		Defense/Small groups		Closing game
	Ball familiarization		Defense/Team		Final sprint
X	Goalkeeper warm-up shooting		Athletics		
			Endurance		

Key:

✖ Cone

▲ Attacking player

● Defense player

Ball box

Foam noodles (foam beams)

Equipment required:
→ 4 foam noodles (foam beams) 4 cones, 1 ball box with sufficient number of handballs, 1 bib

Description:
In this training unit, the initial action – crossing of the center back and the pivot – will be extended by a second pivot from the wing position. After the warm-up consisting of a tag game and a sprint contest, the goalkeeper warm-up shooting already incorporates the required running moves along the 6-meter line. During a series of shots, the players repeat the standard course and afterwards develop a first variant of playing with the second pivot from the wing position and making the relevant decisions in two small group exercises. Finally, the players practice another variant in a team exercise and both variants in a free game.

The training unit consists of the following key exercises:
- Warm-up/Stretching (individual exercise: 10 minutes/total time: 10 minutes)
- Short game (10/20)
- Sprint contest (10/30)
- Goalkeeper warm-up shooting (10/40)
- Offense/Series of shots (10/50)
- Offense/Small groups (15/65)
- Offense/Small groups (10/75)
- Offense/Team (15/90)

Training unit total time: 90 min.

Systematic development of handball offense concepts
Game opening with variants and continuous playing options

No.: 3-1	Warm-up/Stretching	10	10

Course:
- Each player has two handballs.
- The players do different dribbling variants. While doing this, they run along the lines on the gym floor.
- If two players meet, they change one of their handballs without interrupting the dribbling task.

Dribbling tasks:
- The players dribble two handballs at the same time.
- The players dribble two handballs alternately.
- The players dribble with their throwing hand and dribble the second ball with their feet.
- The players dribble with their non-throwing hand and dribble the second ball with their feet.

Afterwards, the players perform stretching/mobilization exercises together.

Systematic development of handball offense concepts
Game opening with variants and continuous playing options

No.: 3-2	Short game	10	20

Course:

- One player is the catcher (1); he is flagged with a bib.
- The coach gives a number as the starting sign (here "3").
- The fleeing players try to make groups according to the given number (B). If a group has the correct number of players, the players of this group cannot be tagged.
- 1 tries to tag a player who missed to join a group.
- He tries to catch (C) the remaining players (D) until he tagged one of them (E). Then he hands over the bib to the tagged player who becomes the next catcher. Afterwards, the coach calls out the next number and the course starts over.

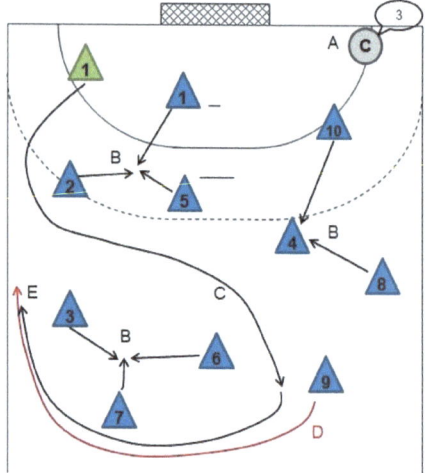

(Figure 1)

(Figure 2: Example for groups of 8)

⚠ The players must always make new groups and get together with other players to make a group during the next course.

⚠ If there are too many (or too few) players in a group, they all may be tagged.

Systematic development of handball offense concepts
Game opening with variants and continuous playing options

No.: 3-3	Sprint contest	10	30

Setting:
- Define a start and a finish line with cones and make two teams.

Course 1 (figure 2):
- The players of the teams stand behind each other at a short distance with their legs in a straddled position.
- The backmost player of each group has a ball and starts from behind the start line.
- 🔺 and 🔺 start simultaneously and run to the foremost player of the group (A).
- As soon as they arrived the foremost player of the respective group, the players start rolling the ball through the straddled legs of their teammates (B).
- The backmost player (now 🔺 / 🔺) picks up the ball and the course starts over.
- After rolling the ball, the players line up at the front of the group.
- The team who crosses the line with all teammates first, gets a point.

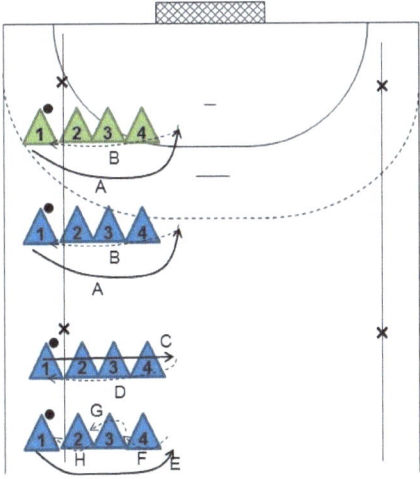

Figure 1

Figure 2

Course 2 (figures 3 and 4):

- The players without a ball lie prone on the floor.
-  and  run (C) over the players on the floor while holding the ball (figure 3); the players on the floor stand up at once afterwards.
- They straddle their legs again and the running player rolls the ball back to the backmost player (figure 4).
- All the players lie down again,  as  the foremost players, and the course starts over.
- The team who crosses the line with all teammates first, gets a point.

(Figure 3)

Course 3:

-  and  start simultaneously and run to the foremost player of the group (E).
- As soon as they arrived, they hand over the ball to the next player through their legs (F).
- This player hands over the ball to the third player above his head (G), the third player hands over the ball to the fourth player through his legs (H), and so on.
- The last player picks up the ball and runs to the foremost player, and so on.
- The team who crosses the line with all teammates first, gets a point.

(Figure 4)

⚠ The players should make sure to maintain a short distance between each other. For course 1 and 3, the players may hold the hips of the respective player in front of them; for course 2, the players may touch the shoulder blade of the respective player in front of them with one hand.

Systematic development of handball offense concepts
Game opening with variants and continuous playing options

No.: 3-4	Goalkeeper warm-up shooting	10	40

Setting:
- Define the shooting position with a foam beam.

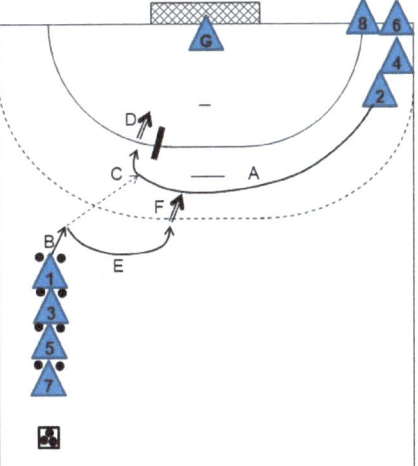

Course:
- ② starts from the wing position and runs along the 6-meter line (A).
- ① has two handballs in the beginning. He makes a slight piston movement (B) and passes one of the balls to ② into his running path (C).
- ② shoots (D) as instructed (top right/bottom right/top left/bottom left).
- ① immediately moves to the center after the pass (E) and shoots at the goal diagonally to the shot of ② (F).
- The course starts over immediately with the next two players.

⚠ The goalkeeper must always start from the center of the goal. He must not move to the respective corner too early.

⚠ During the second part of the goalkeeper warm-up shooting, the players shoot from the right side.

| No.: 3-5 | Offense/Series of shots | 10 | 50 |

Setting:
- Define the break-through area with two foam noodles (foam beams) (see figure).

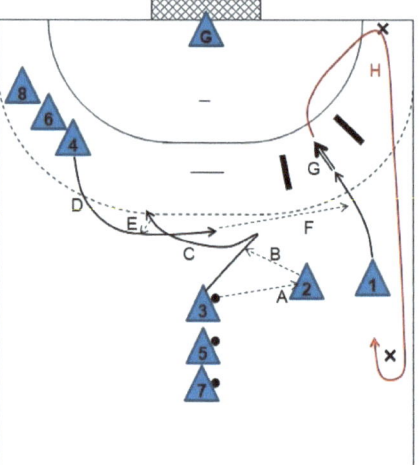

Course:
- 3 plays the initial pass to 2 (A), makes a slight piston movement to the right, and receives a return pass (B).
- 3 clearly moves to the left (C) (he may bounce the ball one time with the hand that is not in direction of the defense).
- 4 starts as the pivot (D), crosses behind 3 (E), and receives a pass.
- 1 starts from the right back position, receives a pass into his running path (F), and shoots at the goal (G).
- After the shot, 1 immediately runs to the cone on the goal line, touches it (H), and runs around the second cone (J).
- While 1 runs around the cones, 5 starts the course over by playing the initial pass to 2 and crossing with 6.
- 1 approaches the goal again, receives a pass after the crossing, and shoots again.

Competition:
- Each player must shoot three times in a row, then the players switch tasks.
- Which players score highest?

⚠ The players must time the initial action in such a way that the pivot does not have to wait for the shooting player after the crossing, but may pass the ball into his running path immediately (i.e. the players must start as soon as the shooting player is on his way to the second cone). The shooting player should observe the initial action himself and run a bit slower around the cones, if necessary.

Systematic development of handball offense concepts
Game opening with variants and continuous playing options

No.: 3-6	Offense/Small groups	15	65

Setting:
- Define the playing fields on the left and right with cones (see figure).

Course 1:
- ▲3 plays the initial pass to ▲4 (A), makes a slight piston movement to the right, and receives a return pass (B).
- ▲3 clearly moves to the left (C) (he may bounce the ball one time with the hand that is not in direction of the defense).
- ▲6 starts as the pivot, crosses behind ▲3 (D), and receives a pass (E).
- ▲3 moves back to the center back position after the crossing (F).
- ▲6 has the ball and moves far to the right after the crossing (G), ▲5 starts from the wing position (H), crosses behind ▲6, and receives the ball (J).
- ▲5 passes to ▲2 at full speed (K), who has started approaching the goal from the left back position (L).
- ▲2 shoots at the goal (M).
- Afterwards, ▲7 starts the next course on the other side and shoots at the goal from the right back position.
- ▲6 stands on the right side in the beginning.

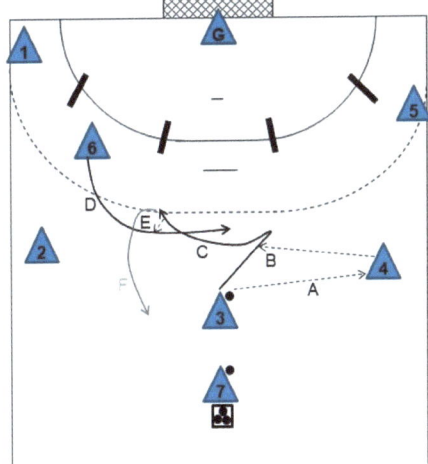

(Figure 1)

(Figure 2)

Course 2:

- The initial action remains the same as in course 1.
- Extend the exercise by adding defense players defending against the left and right back position players.
- 6 has the ball and moves far to the right after the crossing (G), 5 starts from the wing position (H), crosses behind 6, and receives the ball (J).
- 5 passes to 2 at full speed (K), who has started approaching the goal from the left back position (L).

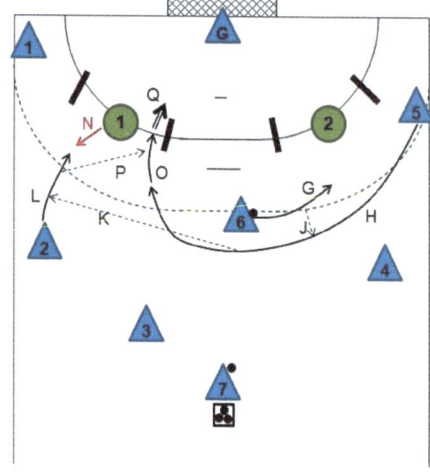

(Figure 3)

- 2 must decide now, depending on the defense position of 1:
    o If 1 remains defensive, 2 shoots from the back position.
    o If 1 makes a step forward (N), 2 passes the ball to 5 (P), who approaches the goal after receiving the pass (O) and finally shoots from within the defined area (Q).
- Afterwards, 7 starts the next course on the other side, i.e. the decision must be made on the right back position.

Systematic development of handball offense concepts
Game opening with variants and continuous playing options

No.: 3-7	Offense/Small groups	10	75

Setting:
- Define the playing fields on the left and right with foam beams (see figure).

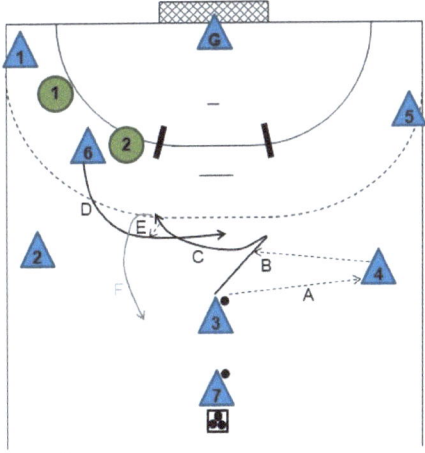

(Figure 1)

Course:
- ③ plays the initial pass to ④ (A), makes a slight piston movement to the right, and receives a return pass (B).
- ③ clearly moves to the left (C) (he may bounce the ball one time with the hand that is not in direction of the defense).
- ⑥ starts as the pivot, crosses behind ③ (D), and receives a pass (E).
- ③ moves back to the center back position after the crossing (F).
- ⑥ has the ball and moves far to the right after the crossing (G), ⑤ starts from the wing position (H), crosses behind ⑥, and receives the ball (J).
- ⑤ passes to ② at full speed (K), who has started approaching the goal from the left back position (L).

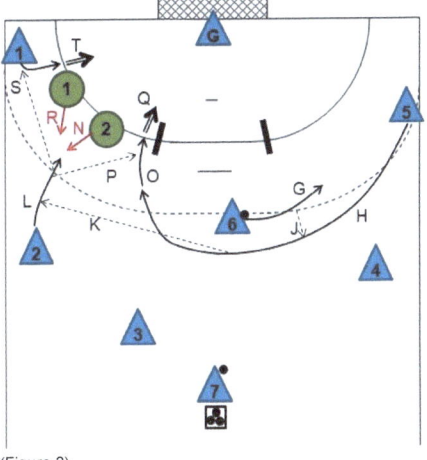

(Figure 2)

- ② must decide now, depending on the position of the two defense players:
    o If both players act defensively, ② shoots from the back position (option 1) or breaks through (option 2).
    o If ② makes a step forward towards ② (N), ② passes the ball to ⑤ (P), who approaches the goal after receiving the pass (O) and finally shoots (Q).
    o If ① makes a step forward or closes the gap (R), ② passes the ball to ① on the wing position (S), and ① shoots at the goal (T).

- Afterwards, ⑦ starts the next course on the other side, i.e. the decision must be made on the right back position. In order to do this, the two defense players move to the other side.

⚠ The back position players should approach the goal vigorously and seek their own opportunities. In parallel, they should observe the behavior of the defense players and decide accordingly (pass to the wing player or the player running behind them).

⚠ Switch the defense players at regular intervals.

Systematic development of handball offense concepts
Game opening with variants and continuous playing options

No.: 3-8	Defense/Team	15	90

Course 1:

- The players play 6-on-6 and implement a variant of the course they practiced before.
- ③ plays the initial pass to ④ (A), makes a slight piston movement to the right, and receives a return pass (B).
- ③ clearly moves to the left (C) (he may bounce the ball one time with the hand that is not in direction of the defense).
- ⑥ starts as the pivot, crosses behind ③ (D), and receives a pass (E).
- When ③ passes the ball to ⑥ (E), ⑤ starts on the wing position and runs along the 6-meter line towards the center at high speed (F) in order to force ⑥ to run along with him (G).

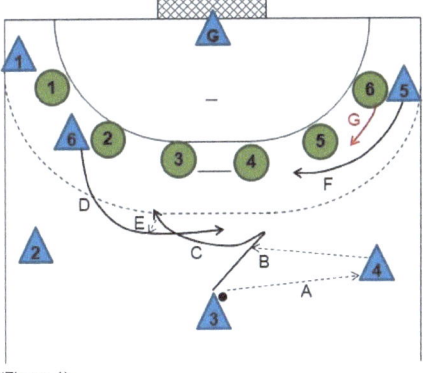
(Figure 1)

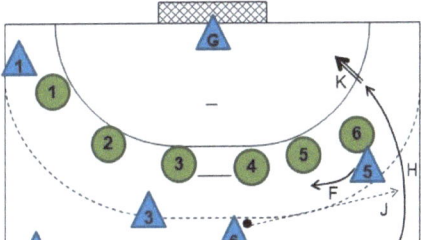
(Figure 2)

- During this running action, ④ moves a bit towards the wing position, then starts to approach the goal at high speed (H), and receives a pass from ⑥ into his running path (J).
- ④ shoots at the goal from the wing position (K).
- Afterwards, the players do the same course on the other side.

⚠ ⑤ must find the right timing for his running action. He must not start too early, because in this case, ⑥ may hand him over to the next defense player and focus on the new wing player.

Course 2:

- The players play 6-on-6.
- The attacking team plays 10 attacks.
  The players always start with the "crossing with the pivot" course and a second pivot from the wing position.
- They may play both variants practiced in the training unit.
- Switch the tasks after 10 attacks. Which team has shot the most goals?

No. 4	Game concept – Crossing of the center back and the pivot plus second pivot from the back position			★★★	90
	Opening part		**Main part**		
X	Warm-up/Stretching		Offense/Individual		Jumping power
	Running exercise	X	Offense/Small groups		Sprint contest
X	Short game	X	Offense/Team		Goalkeeper
	Coordination		Offense/Series of shots		
	Coordination run		Defense/Individual		**Final part**
	Strengthening		Defense/Small groups		Closing game
X	Ball familiarization		Defense/Team		Final sprint
X	Goalkeeper warm-up shooting		Athletics		
			Endurance		

Key:

 Cone

 Attacking player

 Defense player

 Ball box

——— Foam noodles (foam beams)

Equipment required:
→ 1 foam noodle (foam beam) 4 cones, 2 ball boxes with sufficient number of handballs, bibs, middle part of a large vaulting box (if applicable)

Description:
The fourth training unit combines crossing of the center back and the pivot with a second pivot from the back position. After warm-up with ball familiarization and a tag game variant, the players practice the running paths. The subsequent goalkeeper warm-up shooting is followed by several small group exercises, which demonstrate decision options. Afterwards, the players practice the course in a team play against different offensive and defensive defense variants.

The training unit consists of the following key exercises:
- Warm-up with ball familiarization (single exercise: 15 minutes/total time: 15 minutes)
- Short game (10/25)
- Ball familiarization (10/35)
- Goalkeeper warm-up shooting (10/45)
- Offense/Small groups (10/55)
- Offense/Small groups (15/70)
- Offense/Team (20/90)

Training unit total time: 90 min.

| No.: 4-1 | Warm-up with ball familiarization | 15 | 15 |

Course 1:
- The players initially make teams of 3, with one handball per team.
- The teams crisscross through one half of the court and keep passing their ball in the same order (1-2-3-1, and so on).
- While doing this, the players perform different running and passing variants.

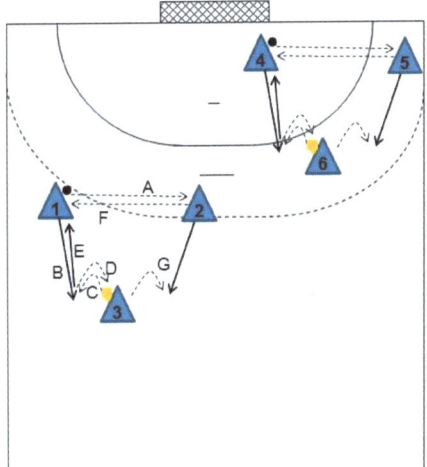

(Figure 1)

Course 2 (see figure):
- Each team has a handball and a bib.
- Two players of the team (one player with the ball) stand in line, the third player stands 2 to 3 meters behind them and holds a bib (see figure).
- 1 passes the ball to 2 (A) and immediately runs backward in direction of 3 (B).
- 3 throws the bib in the air (C), 1 catches it and throws it back again at once (D).
- Then 1 makes a forward piston movement (E), and receives a return pass from 2 (F).
- After the pass, 2 runs backward in direction of 3, receives the bib (G), throws it back, makes a forward piston movement, and the course starts over.
- The other teams do the drill in parallel.
- Since the players cannot play a return pass immediately after receiving the ball (the teammate must first play the double pass with the bib), they fulfill different tasks in the meantime:
    - Dribble the ball around the body.
    - Moving the ball around the hips, feint a pass to the right, feint a pass to the left.
    - Dribble the ball through the legs ("8").
    - Throw the ball in the air and catch it behind the back.
- After 20 passes, switch the tasks within each team of 3.

Extension:
- The players with the bib also fulfill tasks between the double passes with the bib:
    - Hand the bib over from one hand to the other through the legs (figure 2).
    - Throw the bib in the air and catch it.
    - When receiving the return pass, catch the bib with the foot and pick it up from there.

(Figure 2)

Systematic development of handball offense concepts
Game opening with variants and continuous playing options

No.: 4-2	Short game	10	25

Setting:
- Define a rectangle as the playing field using cones and lines on the court floor.
- Make two teams.

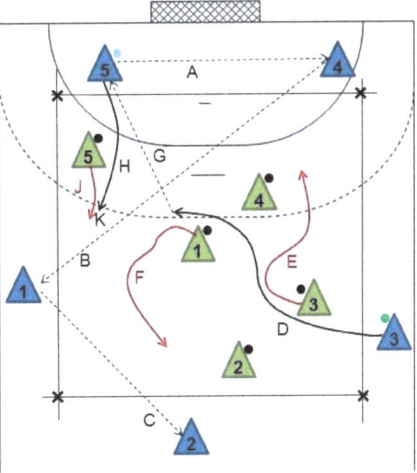

(Figure 1)

Course:
- One team starts in the field. All players of this team each continuously dribble a ball.
- The second team spreads outside of the field, with two handballs of different color (here blue and green).
- The players of the team outside of the field keep playing passes with the blue ball (A, B, and C).
- The player who has the green ball dribbles into the field (D) and tries to tag one of the players in the field while dribbling.
- The players in the field (also dribbling) try to flee and avoid being tagged (E and F).
  The catcher also may pass the ball to another teammate (G) who is currently not in possession of the blue ball.

(Figure 2)

- Afterwards, this player becomes the catcher (H); the former catcher must leave the field.
- As soon as a player has been tagged (J and K), he must sit down for a short while and stand up again. Only after that he may be tagged again.
- The catchers get a point for each player tagged.
- Switch the tasks after five minutes. Who has scored highest?

| No.: 4-3 | **Ball familiarization** | 10 | 35 |

Course:

(Figure 1)

- 2 makes a slight piston movement to the right, and receives a pass from 3 (A).
- 2 clearly moves to the left (B) (he may bounce the ball one time with the hand that is not in direction of the defense).
- 6 starts as the pivot, crosses behind 2 (C), and receives a pass (D).
- 6 passes the ball to 3 into his piston movement path (E).
- During (or shortly after) the crossing, 1 runs to the 6-meter line from the left back position (F).
- 3 passes to 1 (G) and 1 passes to the right wing player 4 (H).
- Immediately after 6 has passed the ball to 3, 6 moves back again to his initial position (J), 2 moves to the left back position (L).
- 3 lines up for the center back position (K) after playing the pass (G).

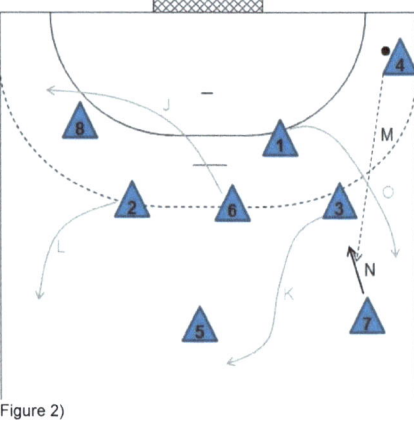

(Figure 2)

- 4 starts the course over on the right wing position by passing the ball (M) to 7 who does the piston movement (N).
- Only after this pass, 1 lines up for the right back position (O).

⚠ The players should get a feel for the right timing of the crossing and when to approach the 6-meter line.

⚠ Also do the course on the other side.

Variant:
- The players pass the ball (G) through a vertically positioned middle part of a large vaulting box.

Systematic development of handball offense concepts
Game opening with variants and continuous playing options

| No.: 4-4 | Goalkeeper warm-up shooting | 10 | 45 |

Setting:
- Put one ball box each on the left and right back positions.

Course:
- ▲1 makes a slight piston movement to the right, and receives a pass from ▲2 (A).
- ▲1 clearly moves to the left (B).
- ▲3 starts as the pivot, crosses behind ▲1 (C), and receives a pass (D).
- ▲3 passes the ball to ▲2 into his piston movement path (E).

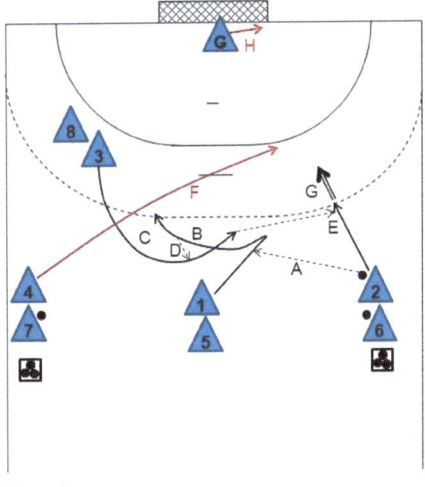

(Figure 1)

- During the crossing, ▲4 moves to the 6-meter line from the left back position (F) and hence confines the inner side of the shooting corridor of ▲2.
- ▲2 makes a stem shot at the right side of the goal as instructed (hands, top, bottom) (G), ▲G starts from the center of the goal and saves the shot (H).
- During the shot, ▲7 starts dribbling on the right back position (K).
- ▲3 runs back to the 6-meter line on the left side after the pass (L), receives a pass in direction of the 6-meter line from ▲7 (M), and shoots at the left side of the goal as instructed (N).
- ▲G tries to save this shot, too (O).
- Afterwards, the players start the next round. In order to do this, ▲1 lines up for the left back position with a ball ( ), ▲2 has moved back to the center back position ( ), ▲4 lines up for the right back position with a ball ( ), ▲3 moves back to the 6-meter line and behind ▲8 ( ).

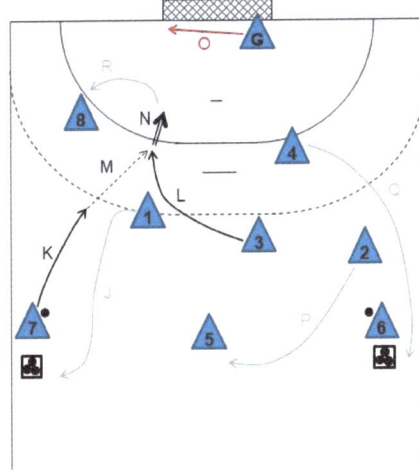

(Figure 2)

Systematic development of handball offense concepts
Game opening with variants and continuous playing options

⚠ The players must time the second shot in such a way that G is able to save the shot. If the shot is delayed, G must start from the center; he is not allowed not wait for the shot in the respective corner.

⚠ Switch the course to the other side after several rounds; i.e. stem shot on the left back position and pivot shot on the right side.

No.: 4-5	Offense/Small groups	10	55

Setting:
- Define the playing field with a foam noodle (foam beam).

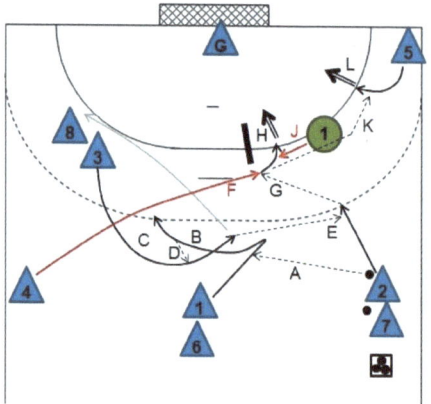

Course:
- 1 makes a slight piston movement to the right, and receives a pass from 2 (A).
- 1 clearly moves to the left (B).
- 3 starts as the pivot, crosses behind 1 (C), and receives a pass (D).
- 3 passes the ball to 2 into his piston movement path (E).
- During (or shortly after) the crossing, 4 moves to the 6-meter line from the left back position (F) and receives a pass from 2 (G).
- 4 must decide now:
   o Shoot, if 1 gives the opportunity for breaking through (H).
   o If 1 closes the gap (J), 4 plays a bounce pass to 5 (K), and 5 shoots at the goal (L).
- Afterwards, the players start the next round. 1 moves to the left back position, 2 moves to the center back position, and 4 lines up for the right back position with a ball. Two pivots do the course alternately; the wing players also take turns.

⚠ 4 should find the right timing for running to the 6-meter line from the left back position.

⚠ The players should repeat the course on the other side as well and start the running move on the right back position.

⚠ Switch the defending player at regular intervals.

Systematic development of handball offense concepts
Game opening with variants and continuous playing options

| No.: 4-6 | Offense/Small groups | 15 | 70 |

Setting:
- Define the playing field with a foam noodle (foam beam).

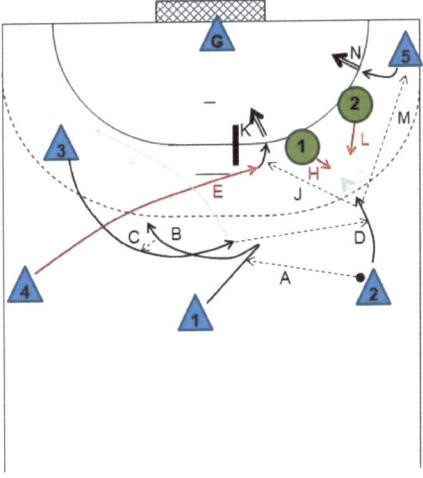

Course (figure 1):
- ▲1 makes a slight piston movement to the right, and receives a pass from ▲2 (A).
- ▲1 clearly moves to the left (B).
- ▲3 starts as the pivot, crosses behind ▲1, and receives a pass (C).
- ▲3 passes the ball to ▲2 into his piston movement path (D).

(Figure 1)

- During (or shortly after) the crossing, ▲4 runs to the 6-meter line from the left back position (E).
- ▲2 must decide now:
  - If both defense players act defensively, ▲2 shoots from the back position (G) or breaks through.
  - If ●1 makes a step forward towards ▲2 (H), ▲2 passes the ball to ▲4 (J), and ▲4 shoots at the goal, if possible (K).
  - If ●2 makes a step forward towards ▲2 (L), ▲2 passes the ball to the wing player ▲5 (M), and ▲5 shoots at the goal, if possible (N).
- If a direct shot is not possible, the players keep playing 3-on-2 until one of them has shot at the goal.

Extension with initial action variant (figure 2):

- The initial action (crossing with the pivot and moving to the 6-meter line from the left back position) remains the same (A, B, C, and E).
- 3 does not play a parallel pass to 2 in this variant, but rather passes the ball directly to 4 (P).
- 4 makes a piston movement towards the gap. If 1 closes the gap, 4 passes the ball to 2 into his parallel piston move (Q), who then breaks through (R) or passes the ball to the wing player (S).
- The players keep playing 3-on-2 freely until one of them has shot at the goal (T).

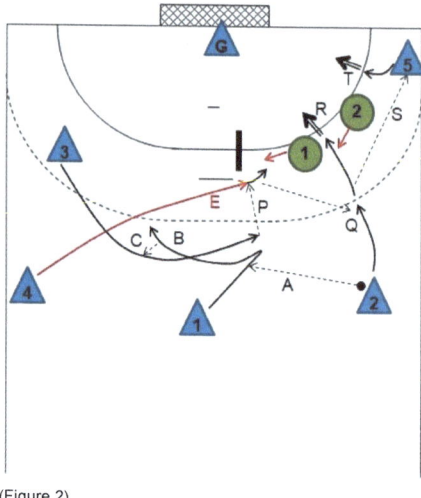
(Figure 2)

Systematic development of handball offense concepts
Game opening with variants and continuous playing options

No.: 4-7	Offense/Team	20	90

Setting (variant 1):
- 6-on-6 game, with a 6-0 defense system.

Course 1:
- The players repeat the course they practiced in the previous exercise, i.e. the center back crosses with the pivot (A to D) and the back position player becomes the second pivot (E).
- The attacking team keeps playing, depending on the behavior of the defense players:
  - If the defense players leave gaps on the right side, 2, who is running along the 6-meter line, may receive a pass (F) and try to get in a good shooting position on the right side, as in exercise 4-6.
  - If the defense players move to the right side (G and H), 4 moves a bit towards the center (K) and passes the ball to 3 into his parallel piston move (L).
  - 3 takes on the position of 2 after the crossing (J).
  - 6 moves back to the 6-meter line (M). The players now try to get in a good shooting position on the left side through interaction of 3, 6, and 1 (N and O).
- Each team plays 10 attacks, then the teams switch tasks.
- Which team has shot the most goals?

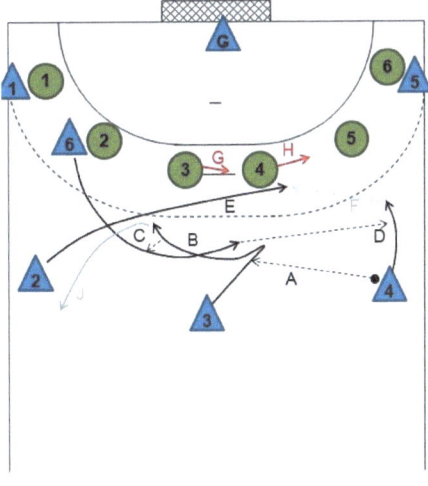

(Figure 1)

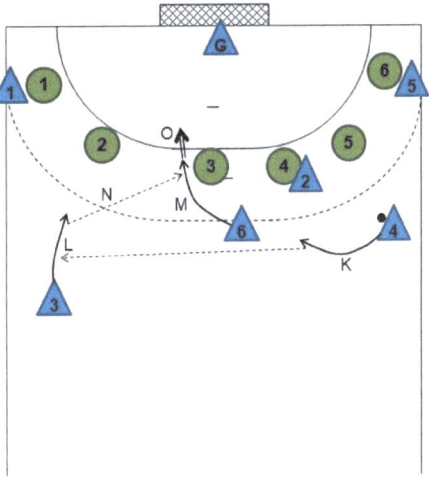

(Figure 2)

⚠ The players should do the initial action both on the right and the left side.

Setting (variant 2):
- 6-on-6 game, with a 5-1 or 3-2-1 defense system.

Course 2:
- Due to the larger gaps, this course with the back position player becoming the second pivot is suitable for playing against more offensive defense systems.
- The players again repeat the course they practiced before; i.e. the center back player crosses with the pivot (A to C), the pivot plays a parallel pass (D), and the back position player becomes the second pivot (E).
    - 3 takes on the position of 2 after the crossing ( ).

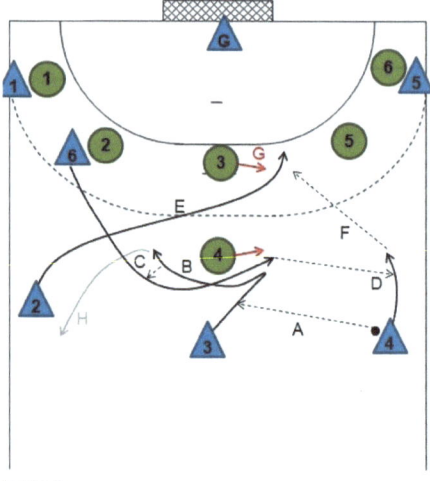

Figure 3

- 4 must decide:
    - Passing the ball to the second pivot (F) and continuous playing on the right side until one of the players is in a good shooting position.
    - If 3 takes over the second pivot 2 (G), 4 must move to the other side (J) and play a parallel pass to 3 (K). 6 moves back to the 6-meter line again, receives the ball (L), and eventually shoots at the goal from the left side (M).

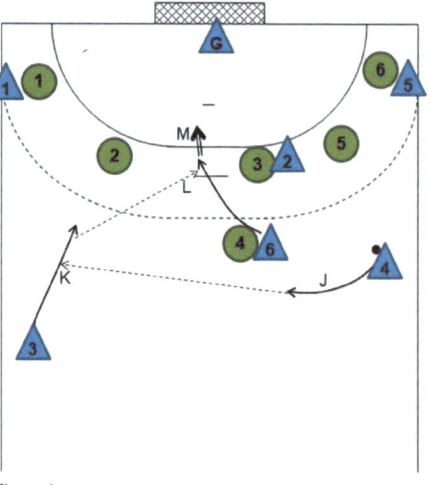

Figure 4

- Each team plays 10 attacks, then the teams switch tasks.
- Which team has shot the most goals?

Course 3:
- The teams again each play 10 attacks.
- The attacks must be started from the center line.
- The coach gives instructions regarding the defense system (6-0, 5-1, or 3-2-1).

Systematic development of handball offense concepts
Game opening with variants and continuous playing options

No. 5	Crossing of the center back and the pivot in outnumbered situations		★★★	90

	Opening part		Main part		Final part
X	Warm-up/Stretching		Offense/Individual		Jumping power
	Running exercise	X	Offense/Small groups		Sprint contest
X	Short game		Offense/Team		Goalkeeper
	Coordination		Offense/Series of shots		**Final part**
	Coordination run		Defense/Individual		
	Strengthening		Defense/Small groups	X	Closing game
X	Ball familiarization		Defense/Team		Final sprint
X	Goalkeeper warm-up shooting		Athletics		
			Endurance		

Key:

  Cone

  Attacking player

  Defense player

  Ball box

| Pole

Equipment required:
→ 2 (4) basketball baskets, 4 poles, 8 cones, 2 ball boxes with sufficient number of handballs

Description:
In this training unit, the players practice crossing of the center back and the pivot as the initial action as well as the different options for the subsequent continuous playing against an outnumbered defense. After the warm-up, the players play two short games in outnumbered situations. This is followed by the goalkeeper warm-up shooting and practicing different outnumbered playing options and decisions. In a free closing game, the players should implement what they practiced before.

The training unit consists of the following key exercises:
- Warm-up with ball familiarization (single exercise: 10 minutes/total time: 10 minutes)
- Short game (20/30)
- Short game (10/40)
- Goalkeeper warm-up shooting (10/50)
- Offense/Small groups (15/65)
- Offense/Small groups (10/75)
- Offense/Team (15/90)

Training unit total time: 90 min.

| No.: 5-1 | Warm-up with ball familiarization | 10 | 10 |

Course:

- Each player has a handball.
- The players run in line from one basket to the next (A) and do exercises with the ball (see tasks).
- In front of the basket, the players pick up their ball and throw it at the board as instructed (B), catch the ball bouncing back (C), and run to the other side (D).

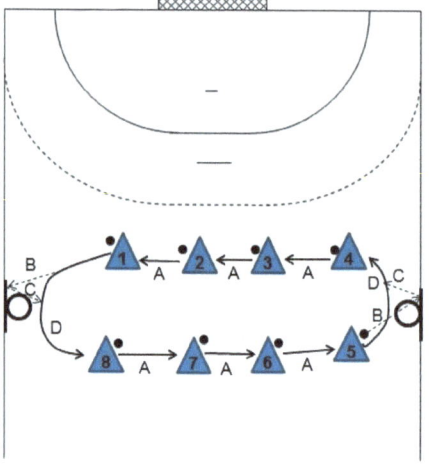

(Figure 1)

Tasks:

- The players dribble the ball with their feet, pick it up in front of the basket, throw it at the board with their throwing hand, and catch it with both hands.
- The players dribble the ball with their feet and rotate their arms in forward direction (backward direction/alternating directions). They throw their ball at the board and catch it with both hands (figure 2).
- The players sidestep and move the handball around their hips in circles. The players throw their ball at the board with both hands and catch it with both hands.

(Figure 2)

- The players run forward and move the handball alternately around their head, hips and knees in circles. Afterwards, they make a jump shot, throw the ball at the board, and catch it with both hands.
- The players run backward while dribbling their ball. They turn around in front of the basket, throw the ball at the board with their non-throwing hand, and catch it with their throwing hand.
- The players run forward while dribbling their ball with their throwing hand. The players throw their ball at the board with both hands and catch it with one hand. While doing this, they should speed up continuously.

Afterwards, the players perform stretching/mobilization exercises together.

Systematic development of handball offense concepts
Game opening with variants and continuous playing options

No.: 5-2	Short game		20	30

Setting:
- This exercise uses the basketball field and both basketball baskets.

Course 1 (figure 1):
- The players play a basketball variant.
- One player (4) must stay under his team's basket and is the center player during his team's next attack.
- 1, 2, 3, and 4 play 4-on-3 against 1, 2, and 3 (A, B, and C) until one player has scored (D) or the attacking players have lost the ball.
- As soon as the attack is over, only three players run back to defend (1, 2, and 3) (E).
- The player who scored (or had the ball right before it was lost (4)), stays under the basket until his teammates start the next attack.

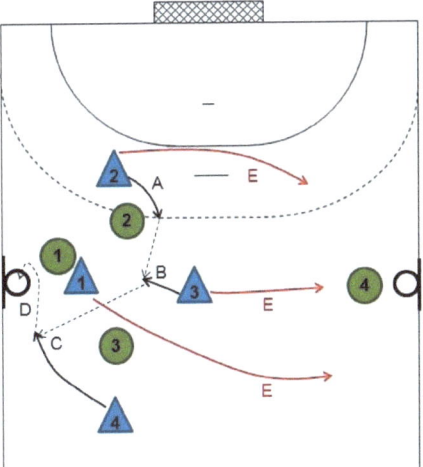
(Figure 1)

(Figure 2)

Systematic development of handball offense concepts
Game opening with variants and continuous playing options

Course 2 (figure 3):
- The players again play a basketball variant.
- The players initially play 4-on-4 (A, B, and C).
- If a player scores (D), he must run around a pole (F), before he is allowed to join his teammates defending.
- The defense hence is outnumbered for a while (E), until the fourth player joins in (G).
- The attacking players should try to take advantage of the outnumbered situation.

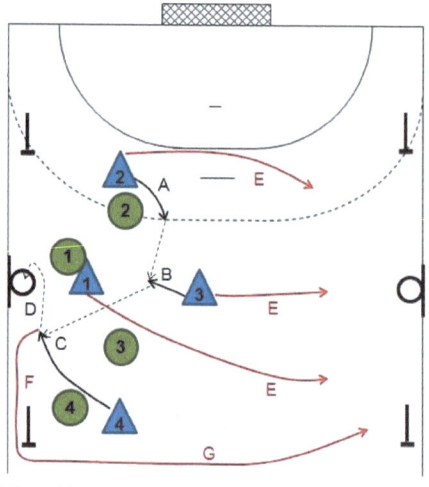

(Figure 3)

⚠️ If there are a many players,
the teams play on two halves of the field in parallel (twice 4-on-4).

⚠️ If there are more than eight but less than 16 players or if there is an uneven number of players, the additional players do the intermediate exercise no. TU 5-2a (all three rounds). After they have fulfilled the tasks, they are substituted and join the basketball game.

| No.: 5-2a | Intermediate exercise for additional players | 20 | 30 |

Course:
- Position two poles for the additional players.

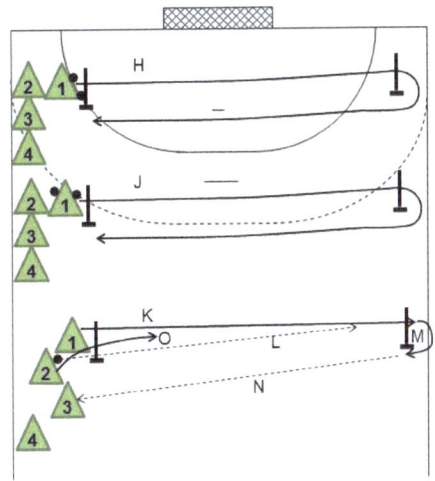

Course 1:
- 1 starts with two balls, runs around the backmost pole and back again (H). While running, 1 dribbles one ball with his feet and moves the other one around his hips in circles.
- Each player must do the exercise one time.

Course 2:
- 1 starts with two balls and dribbles both around the backmost pole and back again (H). Afterwards, 1 hands over the balls to the next player.
- Each player must do the exercise one time.

Course 3:
- 1 sprints to the backmost pole without a ball (K) and receives a pass from 2 into his running path (L). 1 runs around the pole (M) and passes the ball to 3 (N).
- Now 2 starts, and so on, until each player has run one time.

| No.: 5-3 | Short game | 10 | 40 |

Setting:
- Position cones as shown in the figure.

Course:
- Upon the coach's whistle, 1, 2, and 3 start at the foremost cones and do jumping jacks on the spot (A).
- 4, 5, and 6 start simultaneously and do push-ups at the backmost cones (B).
- Upon the next whistle, 1, 2, and 3 start to run to the other side (C) and play 3-on-2 (D, E, and F) against 1 and 2. They should try to lay down the ball behind the line as quick as possible (G).
- Upon the whistle, 4, 5, and 6 move to the foremost cone and start to do the jumping jacks; 7, 8, and 9 start to do the push-ups.
- After the attack, 1 and 2 line up again to become attacking players. The two players who did not lay down the ball become the defense players.

Systematic development of handball offense concepts
Game opening with variants and continuous playing options

| No.: 5-4 | Goalkeeper warm-up shooting | 10 | 50 |

Course 1 (figures 1 and 2):

- ① makes a slight piston movement to the right, and receives a pass from ② (A).
- ① clearly moves to the left. ③ starts as the pivot, crosses behind ①, and receives a pass (B).
- ③ passes the ball to ② into his piston movement (C).
- During the initial action, ④ starts dribbling on the left back position and passes the ball to ⑧ at the 6-meter line (D).
- ⑧ shoots at the left side of the goal as instructed (hands, top, bottom) (E), G starts from the center of the goal and saves the shot (F).
- ③ and ① run to the 6-meter line (G and H).
- Immediately after passing the ball to ⑧, ④ moves backwards to his initial position before he starts the next piston movement.
- He receives a long pass from ② into his running path (J) and passes the ball back to ② into his piston movement path (K).

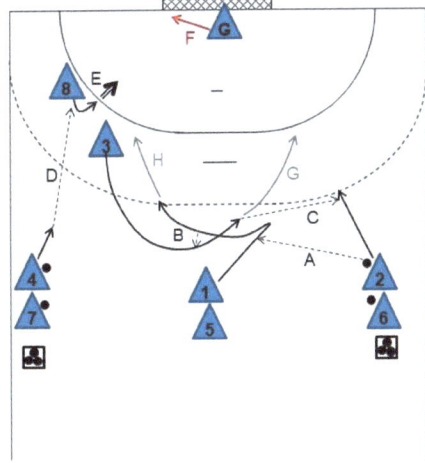
(Figure 1)

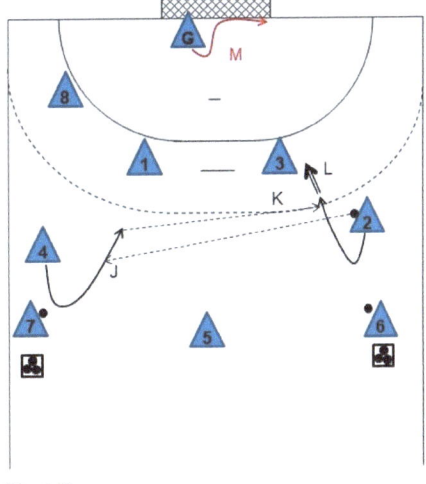
(Figure 2)

- ② makes a stem shot next to ③ and shoots at the right side of the goal as instructed (L).
- G moves back to the center of the goal and tries to save the shot from his initial position (M).
- Afterwards, the players start the next round with crossing of ⑤ and ⑧.
- ① shoots from the pivot position, ⑦ and ⑥ play on the back positions.
- ③ lines up behind ⑥, ④ behind ⑤, and ② behind ⑦.

Systematic development of handball offense concepts
Game opening with variants and continuous playing options

⚠ The exercise is very challenging with regard to timing and passing precision. The players should initially get a feel for the timing and the passes and then speed up their piston movements.

⚠ The players should repeat the course on the other side as well, i.e. pivot shot on the right side and stem shot on the left back position.

Course 2 (figures 1 and 3):
- The initial action, i.e. crossing of the center back and the pivot, piston movement of the left back position player, shot of the pivot (A to H) remain the same.
- ④ moves backwards again to his initial position before he starts the next piston movement.
- ② passes the ball to ④ into his running path (J).
- ④ makes a piston movement towards the goal and passes the ball to ① at the 6-meter line (N), who eventually shoots from the pivot position at the left side of the goal as instructed (O).

(Figure 3)

- Between the two shots, Ⓖ touches the right goalpost (P) before he tries to save the second shot at the left side of the goal (Q).

⚠ The players should repeat the course on the other side as well and shoot from the right side.

Systematic development of handball offense concepts
Game opening with variants and continuous playing options

| No.: 5-5 | Offense/Small groups | 15 | 65 |

Setting:
- Define the playing fields with two poles.

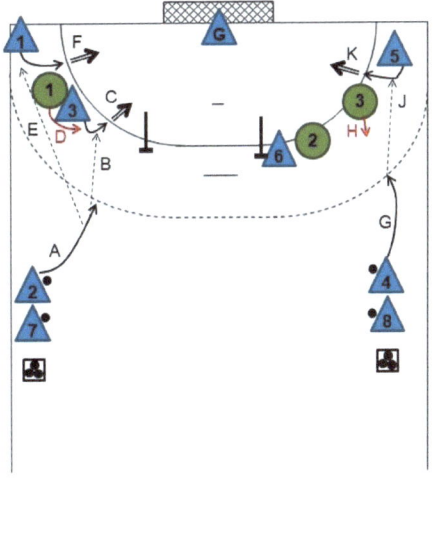

Course:
- ② makes a piston movement towards the pole (A) and decides:
  - If ① stands behind ③, ② passes the ball to ③ at the 6-meter line (B), and ③ shoots at the goal (C).
  - If ① runs around the pivot (D), ② passes the ball to the wing player ① (E), and ① shoots (F).
- After the shot, ④ starts on the right back position with his back turned to the goal, dribbles the ball through his legs, turns around, secures the ball, and then starts approaching the gap between ② and ③ (G).
- Depending on the behavior of the defense players (H), ④ must decide whether he should approach the goal himself, pass the ball to ⑥ or pass the ball to the wing player ⑤ (J).
- The players should either shoot directly (K) or keep playing 3-on-3 freely until one of them has shot at the goal.
- Afterwards, the players start the course over on the left back position.

⚠ Switch the course after some time, so that the player on the right must decide and the 3-on-2 outnumbered situation is to be solved on the left side.

No.: 5-6	Offense/Small groups	10	75

Setting:
- Define the playing field with a pole.

Course:

(Figure 1)

- **3** plays the initial pass to **4** (A), slightly moves to the right, and receives a return pass (B).
- **3** moves to the left (C), **6** crosses behind **3** and receives a pass (D).
- **6** passes the ball to **4** (E). **6** and **3** move to the 6-meter line after the crossing (F and G).
- **4** plays a long pass to **2** into his running path (H).
- **2** must decide now – depending on the behavior of the three defense players:
  - If **2** makes a step forward towards **2** (J), **2** passes the ball to the pivot (L) or to the wing player (M), depending on the position of **1** (K).

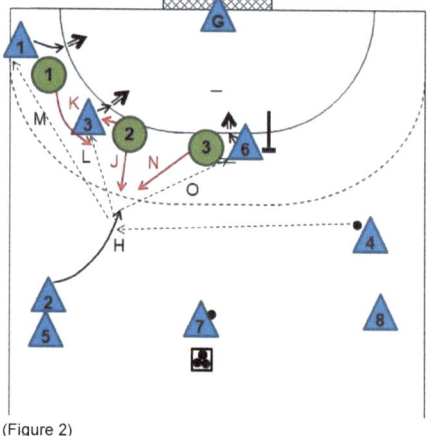

(Figure 2)

  - If **3** makes a step forward (N) and **2** covers the pivot, **2** passes the ball to **6** on the opposite pivot position (O).
- Afterwards, the course starts over with **3** as the pivot and new back position players. **6** lines up for the back position, only the wing player **1** keeps his position or takes turns with a second wing player.

⚠️ **2** should approach the goal at full speed and then make a good decision as quick as possible depending on the behavior of the defense players.

⚠️ The players should repeat the initial action on the other side as well and make the decision on the right back position.

| No.: 5-7 | Closing game | 15 | 90 |

Course:

- The players play 6-on-5. The attacking team plays 11 attacks, then the teams switch tasks. The attacking team wins if they have scored at least seven goals; otherwise the defense players win.
- The losing team must do 10 push-ups and two accelerating runs before the teams switch tasks.
- The attacking players repeat the course they practiced before; i.e. the center back crosses with the pivot (A to E), the center back becomes the second pivot (4-2) (H and J).
- If the defense players do not move along to the right side when ▲6 passes the ball to ▲4 (E), ▲4 may break through or pass the ball to ▲5 on the wing position (F), and ▲5 eventually shoots at the goal (G).
- If the defense players move along to the right side, ▲4 plays a long pass to ▲2 into his running path (K).
- ▲2 must decide, depending on the behavior of the defense players:
    - If ▲2 makes a step forward towards ▲2, ▲2 passes the ball to the pivot (L) or to the wing player (M), depending on the position of ▲1.
    - If ▲3 makes a step forward and ▲2 covers ▲3 at the 6-meter line, ▲2 passes the ball to ▲6 on the opposite pivot position (N) or – if ▲4 obstructs the passing path – back to ▲4 (O), who then tries to take advantage of the outnumbered situation himself.

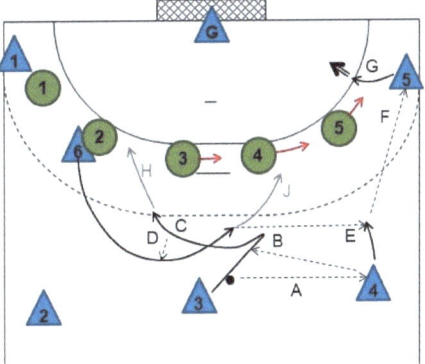
(Figure 1)

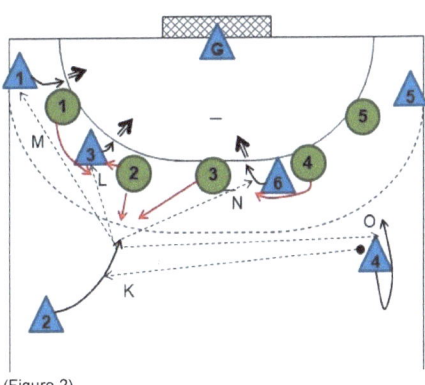
(Figure 2)

⚠ The attacking players should make decisions according to the behavior of the defense players; however, they should play patiently and seek clear scoring opportunities.

⚠ The players should do the course on both sides.

2. Counteractive measures to be expected and appropriate reactions

A. Preventing a pass to the crossing pivot

- One of the most frequent counteractive measures of defense systems that try to interrupt the back position/pivot circle (A bis D) is to directly follow **6** into his crossing movement in order to prevent the pass during the crossing (E).

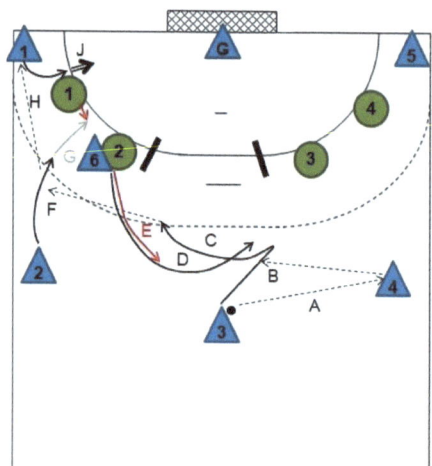

- One variant that can be used against this defense behavior is shown in the exercises TU 1-7 and TU 1-8 of training unit 1.

- The back position player (**2**) who is playing on the side from which **6** starts, does a parallel piston move and directly receives a pass from **3** (F).

- The players then keep playing on the left side until one of them has shot at the goal (G to J).

B. Stepping forward of the defense players on the side where the ball will be passed to after the back position/pivot circle

- The defense players often try to put **6** under pressure, i.e. **4** steps forward towards him and **5** towards **4**.

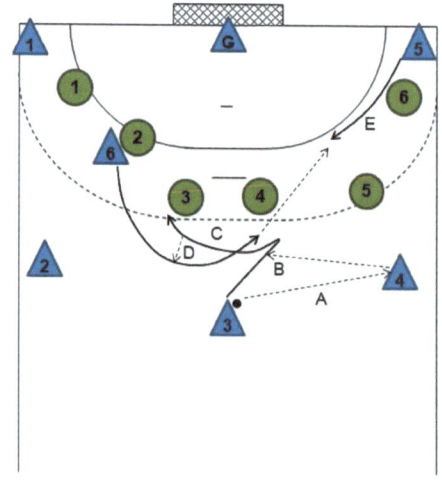

- The attacking players may cope with this behavior by implementing the variant where **5** becomes the second pivot, similar to TU 3 (E).

- Another possible variant would be an "empty crossing" of **4** and **5**.

C. Stepping forward of the defense players towards the player who is about to receive the ball after the back position/pivot circle

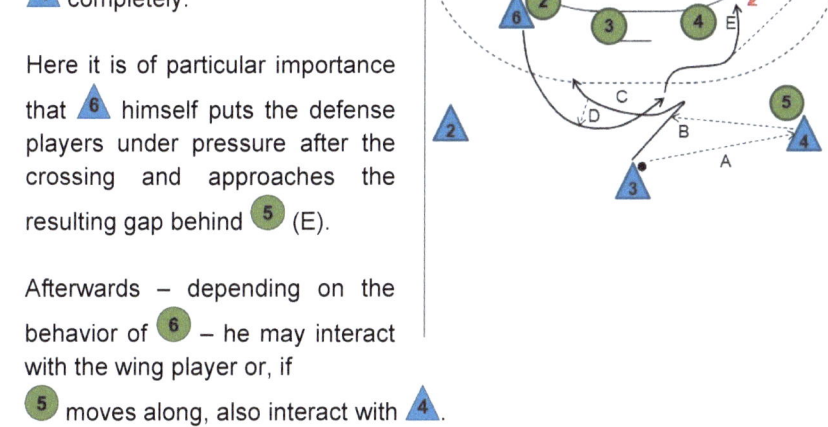

- The defense players often try to put ⑥ under pressure, i.e. obstructing the passing path to ④ completely.

- Here it is of particular importance that ⑥ himself puts the defense players under pressure after the crossing and approaches the resulting gap behind ⑤ (E).

- Afterwards – depending on the behavior of ⑥ – he may interact with the wing player or, if ⑤ moves along, also interact with ④.

- ⑤ may also run around and get past ⑥ as another option. ⑤ should actively join in and always be available to receive passes.

3. About the editors

Felix Linden, born in Tönisvorst/Germany in 1988

Since 2017: Certified DHB young talents' coach for competitive areas

Since 2016: A-License, DHB

Since 2014: Trainer/lecturer at TuS Lintfort, HK Mönchengladbach, TSV Kaldenkirchen, and ATV Biesel (all in Germany)

2010: Assistant coach at TuS Lintfort with promotion to the second national handball league (Germany)

2009: Coach of the female under-19 handball team at Neusser HV (Germany) with qualification for the regional league

Since 2005: Team handball coach

(Photo: Andreas Eykenboom)

Editor's note

I started as a youth coach, of course, and I am still fascinated by team handball. Ever since my aim has been to provide diverse and focused handball training and to help both male and female handball players to develop individually. For me, it is important to provide inspiration to both coaches and players over and over again with my exercises and to improve their skills in a diverse manner. This book is intended to encourage you to develop your own ideas and to introduce them into your training units.

Yours sincerely,

Felix Linden

JÖRG MADINGER, born in Heidelberg (Germany) in 1970

June 2018: 3-day workshop: „Welcome to Füchse Berlin – Top-class handball and "practiced" youth development", held by the **German Handball Association (Deutscher Handballbund, DHB)**

July 2014: 3-day coaching workshop: "Basic components of goalkeeper training", held by the **DHB**

May 2014: 3-day coaching further training during the VELUX EHF Final4, **German Handball Coaching Association (Deutsche Handball Trainer Vereinigung, DHTV)/DHB**

May 2013: 3-day coaching further training during the VELUX EHF Final4, held by the **DHTV/DHB**

Since July 2012: A-License, DHB

Since February 2011: Handball club trainings, coaching (training and competitive areas)

November 2011: Foundation of the Handball Specialist Publishing Company (Handball Fachverlag) (handall-uebungen.de, Handball Practice and Special Handball Practice)

May 2009: Foundation of the handball online platform handball-uebungen.de

2008-2010: Youth coordinator and youth coach, SG Leutershausen (Germany)

Since 2006: B-License

4. Further reference books published by DV Concept

From warm-up to handball team play – 75 exercises for every handball training unit

By making your training units more diverse, you can increase the players' motivation, since you consistently offer new approaches to improve and refine familiar movement sequences. In this book, you will find inspiring exercises you can apply during each phase of your everyday team handball training – from warm-up and goalkeeper warm-up shooting to the common contents of the main phase and the closing games. Each exercise is illustrated and described in an easy, comprehensible manner. Specific notes give you tips on what you need to be aware of.

This book deals with the following key subjects:

Warm-up:
- Basic warm-up
- Short warm-up games
- Sprint contests
- Coordination
- Ball familiarization
- Goalkeeper warm-up shooting

Basic exercises, basic play, and target play:
- Offense/series of shots
- General offense
- Fast throw-off
- 1st and 2nd wave
- Defensive action
- Closing games
- Endurance

Minihandball training and handball training for young kids (5 training units)

Minihandball training and handball training for kids is different from minihandball training for older players and considerably different from handball training for competitive players. During their first contact with "handball", kids should be familiarized with the ball in a playful way. They should be taught that being active, doing sports, playing together, and even playing against each other is fun.

This book contains a short introduction to handball for kids and young children and its special characteristics as well as example exercises which help to make your training units interesting and more diverse.

Following this, there are five complete training units of different difficulty levels that focus on the basic handball techniques (dribbling, passing, catching, shooting, and defending in a game with opponents). The kids are playfully introduced to the subsequent handball-specific basics. At the same time, particular attention is payed to general physical experience and the development of coordination skills.

The exercises are illustrated and described in an easy, comprehensible manner. They can be immediately integrated in every training unit. By using the given training variants, you can easily adjust the difficulty level of the training units to the respective target group. The variants should also encourage you to modify and further develop the exercises to make each training unit a new and more diverse experience for the children.

Varied handball shooting drills - 60 exercises for every handball training unit

Shooting is a central component of team handball and must be practiced and improved regularly. Therefore, it is reasonable to integrate shooting series into training units from time to time. This collection of exercises contains 60 comprehensible practical drills focusing on this subject. They can be integrated in every training unit.

The exercises are divided into the following six categories and three difficulty levels (easy, medium, difficult):
Technique, Shooting at fixed targets, Series of shots at the goal, Shooting training for specific playing positions, Complex series of shots, Shooting competitions

Competitive games for your everyday handball training - 60 exercises for every age group

Handball needs quick and correct decisions in each game situation. This can be trained playfully and diversely through handball-specific games. These 60 exercises are divided into seven categories and train the playing skills.

The book deals with the following subjects:
Team ball variants, Team play with different targets, Tag games, Sprint and relay race games, Ball throwing and transportation games, Games from other types of sports, Complex closing game variants

Training of defensive and semi-offensive cooperative defense strategies for handball teams - (60 exercises – From 1-on-1 to small group and team defense)

A good defense is a prerequisite for modern team handball. The intention is not only to prevent goals but also to actively win the ball and subsequently initiate a fast attack. The offense should permanently be put under pressure and forced to make mistakes.

The exercises in this collection initially deal with the individual basics of defense play. Individual and position-specific training marks the starting point for subsequent cooperative defense play and allows for choosing the appropriate defense system. The basics both include exercises on legwork, 1-on-1 defense and covering the pivot in combination with fast adjustment to subsequent actions as well as blocking and anticipating on the wing positions of a proactive defense system.

The second part of the collection deals with cooperative small group defense play and focuses on handing over/taking over attacking players along the defense line (width of defense) and on making agreements when defending against the pivot.

The third chapter introduces cooperative team defense in 6-0, 5-1, 3-2-1, and 4-2 defense systems along with possible variants.

Handball Practice 11 – Extensive and diverse athletics training

This book contains the following training units:
- TU 1 – Series of shots with reflexive jumping power training
- TU 2 – Intensive speed strength/speed strength endurance training with various running directions
- TU 3 – Handball-specific endurance training with fast break movements
- TU 4 – Intense athletics training for arms and legs
- TU 5 – Handball-specific endurance training in game-like situations

Handball Practice 14 – Interaction of back position players with the pivot – Shifting, Screening, and Using the Russian Screen

This book contains the following training units:
- TU 1: Individual training for the pivot – Pushing through the defense with the Russian screen
- TU 2: Pivot – Achieving positional advantages in small-group team play
- TU 3: Improving the interaction of back position players with the pivot
- TU 4: Small group game: Piston movement / countermovement of the back position players and interaction with the pivot
- TU 5: Acting against the defending wing position player with a physically stronger pivot

For further reference and e-books visit us at:
www.handball-uebungen.de